THIRD

MW01505839

# Collect What You Produce

## How You Can **Get More Patients**, **Accelerate Your Cash Flow**, and **Crush Your Accounts Receivable**

# CATHY JAMESON, PhD

ISBN-13: 978-1-7325624-4-8
ISBN-10: 1-7325624-4-X
Library of Congress Control Number: 2019910964

Designed by Joni McPherson, mcphersongraphics.com
Edited by Kristen C. Forbes

Cathy Jameson, PhD
Post Office Box 488
Davis, OK
405-842-7711

# TESTIMONIALS

*"Collect What You Produce remains an insightful exploration into the opportunities and challenges that businesses face about financing dental care. Cathy's practical guidance will inform practitioners and business managers in navigating the complexities of effectively interacting with patients around financial matters—while creating trust-based relationships for any practice's success."*

**Stanley M. Bergman**
Chairman of the Board and Chief Executive Officer
Henry Schein, Inc.

*"Cathy Jameson is a true visionary and pioneer in the business and management of dentistry. Having known her for over 20 years, I feel her business philosophy and simple approach to team success is essential and inspirational reading for every dental practice whether large or small. She is a dynamo and her positive energy translates throughout her book...especially on stage and in your practice. It is a must read."*

**Dr. Larry Rosenthal**
Apa Rosenthal Group, New York City, New York
Director of the Aesthetic Advantage Continuum at NYU

*"Dr. Cathy Jameson's impact on our team in general and on me personally has been colossal. Her success systems and guidance led to a level of financial health and profitability that was unthinkable a few years prior. Every high achiever can benefit from coaching. Don't miss out on this book of wisdom from this treasured visionary!"*

**Dr. Mark Hyman**
Adams School of Dentistry
University of North Carolina, Chapel Hill
Greensboro NC

*"My team and I have been blessed to have been taught from the best of the best about finances, Cathy Jameson. She made us realize that when you create value for the care a patient needs and wants, finding the right financial solution is simply a partnership discussing money... a much more rewarding approach than taking on an adversarial role. Thank you for helping us be more successful."*

**Dr. Jill Wade**
Stonebriar Dental Design and Relevance Total Health
Frisco, Texas

*"From day one I applied Cathy's systems and principles in my practice. With her strong belief in goals and communication it becomes natural to build a comfortable and successful journey from diagnosis to financial agreement to treatment. Even in tough economic times, by sticking to the principles in CWYP we have been able to maintain and grow. By working "smarter, not harder" I have a successful, twenty-year practice full of "forever patients" thanks to Cathy."*

**Dr. Shannon Griffin**
President, Oklahoma Dental Association

*"Having been a client of Jameson Management for many years, I appreciate the value of the systems they teach to consistently practice at an optimal level. I approached Jameson at a critical time. I was midcareer, successful, and busy but I was burned out, stressed, and working too hard with no time for family or leisure.*

*The Jameson consultants taught us systems and skills so that we could work smarter, with less stress while delivering excellent customer service and clinical care. Our days were scheduled to maximize our efforts and at the same time we increased our production.*

**Dr. Chuck Norman**
Greensboro, NC
Past president of the American Dental Association

*"Count me a fan of Cathy Jameson. Her depth of expertise and experience is nothing short of astounding. Keep her book close to you and refer to it often. It will make a tremendous difference in your success—and your well-being."*

**Penny Reed**
Memphis, TN
Author of Growing Your Dental Business

*"It doesn't matter how much you can produce, if you can't get it collected! And, nobody wants to strong-arm patients in a dental or healthcare setting… so how do you do it? You're holding the answer in your hand. Dr. Cathy Jameson shares the secrets from practical application, coaching experience, and years of success in converting production to collections. This is the information you need to deliver high-level patient care, develop a top-notch, well-paid team, and enjoy your own success as a dental professional."*

**Katherine Eitel-Belt**
Founder, LionSpeak
Master Speaker, Trainer and Coach

# DEDICATION

I dedicate this 3rd Edition of COLLECT WHAT YOU PRODUCE to the many people who have carved the path for the amazing service of patient financing in the dental world. You have diligently worked to make this service available to both patients and practices alike.

I dedicate this 3rd Edition of COLLECT WHAT YOU PRODUCE to the coaches, advisers and clients who have supported me and my teaching throughout my career. Thank you.

I dedicate this 3rd Edition of COLLECT WHAT YOU PRODUCE to my favorite dentist—and beloved husband, friend, and colleague, Dr. John Jameson. You are the nicest person I have ever known. You are nice to all people—all the time, including me. (And that's not always easy!) You have provided steadfast support—always! You're THE BEST!

And, I dedicate this book to Carrie Jameson-Webber and Jess Webber. I am grateful to the two of you for believing in the mission of Jameson Management and for carrying on the legacy that John and I began. Thank you for your steadfast courage, determination, and entrepreneurial spirit. You move the organization forward with integrity, insight, and commitment to values. Truly, you are helping people live "healthy, happy lives—whatever that means to them." I love you.

# TABLE OF CONTENTS

# FOREWORD

**M**y career into dentistry wasn't planned...in fact, I was somewhat dental phobic! When entering into the dental profession, and needing to get on the fast track of becoming a business dental expert, I sought out dental industry publications, study clubs, and lectures, and applied the principles to what I knew from the corporate business world. It was in my search that I found Cathy Jameson presenting on *Great Communication = Great Production* and purchased her book on the spot. Absolute game changer for me, the practice and the study club we started. I consider the 1st edition of *Collect What You Produce* timeless and the framework of my dental career. Foundational business principles don't change, but everything else does...and this new book is just in time to address the new challenges facing businesses today. As dental business leaders and owners, tools like this book may be the guide you need and are searching for to get from where you are profitability-wise in your practice to where you want to be.

Today, not only is Cathy one of my mentors, but I'm most proud of her being a lifetime friend. May you take advantage of the knowledge provided by Dr. Cathy Jameson.

**Bete Johnson**
Senior Vice-President and General Manager
Care Credit

*Bete Johnson is an expert in relationship development and management. As Senior Vice President, GM of Dentistry at CareCredit, Bete continues to identify and develop partnerships and manages more than 1,300 professional meetings and tradeshows a year, creating the opportunity to enhance practice engagement and training for the sales organization. Bete has been recognized for her impact on the healthcare community with the Linda Miles Spirit Award, the Nash Institute Partnering Professional Award and has been identified as a Top 25 Woman in Dentistry by Dental Products Report. She currently serves on the Board of Directors for the Speakers and Consultants Network (SCN). A native Californian, Bete lives with her husband of 35 years in Orange County where they raised three collegiate athletes.*

# PREFACE

*"If your actions inspire others to dream more, learn more, do more, and become more, you are a leader."*

— John Quincy Adams

D o you think of yourself as a leader? Well, I do. If you are on a team, of any kind, including a dental team, you are a leader. No matter what your role, you are a leader.

**First**, you are a leader of yourself. Each day, every day, you decide how you will approach the day. You decide about the attitude you will bring to the day. You decide if you will be an asset to the organization—or not! You decide if you will exert extra effort to create and maintain happy patients so they will accept recommendations, follow through with treatment, stay with the practice, and refer others to you. You choose. As a leader of yourself, you decide how you will impact each day—and, ultimately, the productivity of your practice.

**Second**, each person is a leader of teammates. Teammates must be able to count on one another. Your colleagues need to trust that you will do what you are supposed to do, when and how you are supposed to do it. And, you have to count on your teammates in the same way. The systems of the practice are so intertwined that if one person—one system—isn't working well, everything bottlenecks! Accountability determines the smoothness of operation, the control of stress, and the ultimate productivity of the practice. Helping each other makes it possible for the days to run smoothly and successfully. Everyone wins.

**Third**, you are a leader of patients. You cannot—nor would you want to—push a patient into making a decision. However, you can lead them into making a decision—one that is good for them: a decision to accept the treatment that the doctor is recommending for them, treatment that will help them to be healthier or more attractive, or both. Your interaction with patients will influence their opinion of your team, your employer, and your organization. You ARE the face of the organization with each and every interaction. This is called ENGAGEMENT. Engagement is considered the most important factor in businesses in the 21st century. Engaged team members create and retain engaged patients. And engaged team members accept the role of leader and the privileges that come with that role.

# TWO TYPES OF LEADERSHIP

## Transactional Leadership

In a work environment where the leadership style is transactional, the leader dictates down to the rest of the team what, when, and how they will do everything. The leader outlines requirements, results that are expected, and rewards. There is little interactive communication. Creativity is not encouraged. Rewards are defined by money, not fulfillment or growth. Rewards for work well done are finite. There's not much room for personal development.

Transactional leadership is a hierarchical style of leadership with a top-down style of authority. The employee does not participate in decision making, nor are their ideas encouraged. Communication channels between executives and employees is limited.

Wow! That doesn't sound fun, does it? Certainly, there are times and situations where the executive team or owners must "take charge," and of course they expect and require certain levels of performance. There are times when transactional leadership is necessary. However, the methods by which leaders encourage productive performance are changing.

## Transformational Leadership

In contrast, transformational leaders inspire and motivate employees to achieve excellent results in their work and to become leaders themselves. This leadership style is horizontal rather than hierarchical. Workers are empowered, and individual goals as well as organizational goals are aligned with their unique talents and abilities.

Transformational leaders consistently stimulate an awareness of the mission and vision of the organization. Open communication is encouraged. Team members are encouraged to participate in creating and writing practice goals and to design action plans to accomplish them. In other words, team members participate—and love it. Engagement is encouraged.

# A GREAT DENTAL TEAM

My definition of a great dental team is "a team of leaders working cohesively toward a common set of goals." Together, as a team of leaders—

each person believing in the service you are providing for patients, believing in the value of the treatment you are providing, and believing in each other—you can build your "IDEAL PRACTICE."

Do the following:

1.  Put excellent systems into place, including financial systems.

2.  Make sure that all team members are fully and completely instructed in how to manage and administer those systems.

3.  Monitor each system to make sure the goals that have been set are being achieved. If they aren't, then as leaders, make necessary adjustments to get things into proper order.

That's how great teams (and practices) function and function well.

So, now leaders, let's find out how to Collect What You Produce!

# CHAPTER ONE

# The Psychology of Money

*"Money is not an end in itself. It is merely a tool to help us achieve some particular goal. If the way we handle our money conflicts with our personal values, we are not going to wind up living happy and fulfilled lives."*

— David Bach, Author of *Smart Women Finish Rich*

**M**oney. That word means many different things to different people. Money—or even the thought of money—stimulates various emotions. Some positive. Some negative.

Take a moment right now and write down the word *money*. Now, underneath, write out every word that comes to your mind when you think of money, including emotional words related to your thoughts regarding money.

## MONEY:

_____

_____

_____

How many words were positive?

How many were negative?

Now ask yourself, what triggered these responses? Where did these thoughts and/or emotions come from?

Let's use this reflection as we take a deep dive into a study of money—and the entire concept of Collect What You Produce. We may find ways to collect even more by producing even more.

> *"In fact, what determines your wealth is not how much you make but how much you keep of what you make."*
>
> — David Bach, Author of *The Automatic Millionaire*

# Money and Psychology? Do They Go Together?

People work hard for their money. Money is the vehicle by which safety and security are obtained, in many ways. Without safety and security, a person is placed into a state of fright and "insecurity," which leads to a state of disequilibrium. No one can function at full capacity in that kind of state, and team members and patients cannot make major decisions properly when money is a major issue of concern.

It is to everyone's benefit that we learn how to turn this area of concern into a comfortable pathway to health, happiness, and stress relief.

# A Healthy Work Environment

Practices that are financially healthy are—usually—happier. Practices that are constantly under financial constraints are—usually—stressed. This stress, when left unbridled, can harm the interpersonal relationships of people on the team. It can negatively affect feelings toward patients. It can affect treatment planning and, thus, every system down the line. When one system begins to falter, there is a domino effect. All other systems begin to falter as well. Money is related to almost every area of the practice and to the people within it.

Can you develop a healthy relationship with money? Yes. Might it take some work? Perhaps. Remember that money is a vehicle. It's not money that you want or need. It's what money will do for you. It is a vehicle. Therefore, take some time to consider what is important to your life and to your ultimate happiness.

For example, if you say, "We need to increase our production. We need to see more patients or do more treatment."

Look deeper. Why do you want to produce more? Is it the increased revenue, the actual money to be exchanged that will bring you pleasure? What will you gain from the increase?

Will you get to:

- do more of the procedures you love to do?
- have more take-home money for your family needs?
- take more time off to spend with family or on personal interests?
- fund your kid's college education?
- pay your team in a more equitable manner?
- fund a retirement program for you and your team?
- pay the bills on time?

In this list, it isn't the money that is the "goal." The money—the increased production—is the means to the end; it is the vehicle.

## Money: An Exchange of Value

Money is an exchange of value. Patients receive the value of health, well-being, improved appearance, keeping their teeth for a lifetime, comfort, and function. Life enhancing benefits. You receive money as the patient's part of the exchange.

Money's value to you and your patients lies in the fact that it serves as an exchange of value for life enhancement. Both you and your patients benefit from an equitable exchange of value which occurs when you feel good about the money you receive for services rendered, and your patient feels good about the investment they made in you and your care.

# CHAPTER TWO

# YOUR IDEAL PRACTICE. WHY NOT?

*"Specificity transforms a vague dream into concrete, achievable goals. If you can practically see, hear, feel, and smell a goal, the chances are excellent that you'll not only know what's required to make it real, you'll actually do what's required to make it real."*

**— David Bach, Author of *The Latte Factor***

What do you see as your "ideal" workplace? I use the word "ideal" on purpose. Why would you settle for anything less than the "ideal?" You deserve to have the practice (or the job) of your dreams—whatever that is to you. Life is way too short and way too precious to "settle."

## CONCEIVE, BELIEVE, ACHIEVE

A VISION STATEMENT is a clear mental and emotional picture of what you want your practice to be like—in an ideal state. The vision of your ideal practice will evolve and change just as you will alter and change throughout time. That's just fine. However, one steadfast aspect of your vision is that it will be grounded upon the MISSION of your practice—the purpose you are serving. Is the Mission Statement for your business related to money and COLLECTING WHAT YOU PRODUCE? YES!

Your Mission Statement is a written declaration of your purpose. It is a statement of who you are, what you do, and a testament of "why" what you do is important. It's your "benchmark." If you believe passionately about your mission and are devoted to bringing it to fruition, there can and will be a financial reward. A reward for work well done.

On the other hand, if you and your team are not passionate about the purpose you are serving, and if there is no "why" that engages your heart, then a financial reward may be absent or may have no healthy meaning to you.

---

**Purpose is a driving force in a person's heart—in and out of the workplace. When people believe in what they are doing, are passionate about the service provided, and find fulfillment and joy in the work being provided, abundance will follow.**

---

Here is an example of the Mission Statement of one of our long-term clients, Dr. Mark Hyman of Greensboro, NC.

- **Dr. Mark Hyman:** "Our mission: We are a team of compassionate, dedicated professionals who provide optimal dental care using state of the art technology. We are enthusiastic in our commitment to you, to excellence and to building relationships within our community."

When you are in the process of making any decision related to your business, ask yourself, "Will this decision support our mission?" The answer must be "yes." If the answer is "no" or "I'm not sure," go back to the drawing board.

## VISION

Once you have developed your Mission Statement, focus on your future—your VISION. Your vision identifies the things you want to bring into a state of reality. When you focus on the things you sincerely and passionately desire, these things come to pass.

The first step to achieving the "ideal" is to define what that looks like to you. Be as specific as possible so that you can visualize what your ideal looks like, feels like, and sounds like. This becomes the beginning of your own strategic plan. It is the pathway to your abundant success.

A strategic plan has three parts:

1.  Where are you now? (Your present situation)

2.  Where do you want to go or what do you want to achieve? (Your vision)

3.  How are you going to get there? (Your goals or your action plan)

Here are some important questions to consider as you develop your "vision"—the future focus of your Healthy Work Environment—YOUR "IDEAL" PRACTICE.

*   What do you want?

*   What kind of service do you want to provide?

*   How do you want to provide that service?

*   What do you want your clients to experience each time they encounter your organization? (Describe your ideal client experience from the initial contact throughout their experience with you.)

*   What kind of team do you want?

*   What are their characteristics and how do they interact with each other, with you, and with your clients?

*   What is your facility/workplace like?

*   What kind of technology do you have? How are you maximizing it?

*   How much do you want to produce and collect?

*   What is your gross and take-home income?

*   What is your reputation in your industry or profession, community, state, country, and/or world? When people think about your organization—or about you personally—what do they think? If someone is seeking your product or service, do they think about you? Do they know how to contact you? Are you easily accessible?

Once you have outlined and imagined this "ideal" business, ask these questions:

- "Do I have this now?"

  If the answer is yes, pat yourself and your team on the back for work well done. Then ask, "How can we do everything we are doing even better?" (There is the ultimately productive question!) If your answer was, no—then ask yourself:

- "What do I need to do to make this happen?"

  Develop a plan of action for altering those things that need improvement.

You may find upon answering these questions that your existing systems are not functioning in a way that supports your new vision. That will not be unusual, nor is that catastrophic! You can implement healthy change that will move you closer to your ideal. **Don't let anything or anyone prevent you from having your ideal business or workplace. You can have it and deserve it.**

(Dr. Mark Hyman and Team, including his coach!)

# HOWEVER!

How can you or anyone who works with you strive toward the ideal if the vision is not clearly defined? The more clearly you describe your ideal and the more the team sees the doctor's commitment to that ideal, the more likely they will be to move toward it. The entire team will respond more full-heartedly! This is good leadership. The following quote is one of my favorites by Peter Senge, the founding chair of the Society of Organizational Learning and author of *The Fifth Discipline.*

## SHARED VISION

*"A shared vision is a force in people's hearts, a force of impressive power. It may be inspired by an idea, but once it goes further—if it is compelling enough to acquire the support of more than one person—then it is no longer an abstraction. It is palpable. People begin to see it as if it exists. Few if any forces in human affairs are as powerful as shared vision."*

— Peter Senge

## JOHN'S IDEAL PRACTICE

I'll never forget the day my husband, John, wrote and shared his vision of his "ideal" dental practice with us—his team. (I was working in the practice at that time.) We had been going through rough financial times during the oil crisis in Oklahoma and were struggling—really struggling. John practiced in a very small town in rural Oklahoma and the major industry at that time was oil. Sounds great, right? But, we did not have the corporate offices or the executives of those oil companies in our area; we had great, salt of the earth folks—the oil field workers. We also had farmers, ranchers, teachers, small business owners and employees, etc., as patients. When the oil crisis hit and the price of oil nose-dived, people moved out of our area in droves.

We were having 50-75 families move out of the area every month. For a small-town business, this was devastating. No one moving in, and hordes of people moving out. Our growing, thriving small town practice slowly and steadily began to go downhill.

Expenses went on. John didn't want to release his team members—he cared deeply for them and their families. But paying them had become difficult. Bills kept coming in—but the money to pay those bills didn't. The more stressed he became at work, the more stressed he became at home. We were on the verge of bankruptcy and on the verge of divorce. When John didn't feel good about himself, he didn't feel good about his practice. He was difficult for his team, and he was unhappy with me. The connectivity of happiness at work and happiness at home was brought to light for us in a personal and very painful manner.

But, just when we thought we were going to lose it all, John and I heard a speaker who talked about VISION and goal setting.

We thought "What could it hurt? Can't get any worse!" So, John wrote out his vision for himself as a dentist, for his patients, his team, his practice, his family, and his legacy. He called a team meeting. We sat in his private office while he read his first "vision statement" to us. It was so beautiful that we all cried—cried because we were so touched by his honesty and his clarity of vision. We went right to work to bring that vision into a state of reality.

We worked hard—diligently and with dedication—to improve everything we were doing. We re-engineered every system in our practice. We worked on communication skills, marketing, and customer service. We listened to people to find out what they needed and how we could serve them better. We met regularly, as a team, to brainstorm ways to improve. And, we always paused to celebrate the small victories along the way—with words of appreciation, notes, and other ways to say "Hey, good job. Thanks."

Over the next year, we increased our business by 50%, and the work we did to build our own business became the foundation of a larger business: Jameson Management, Inc., a corporation focused on helping others find ways to build productive, profitable, stress-controlled businesses that support people in a healthy, fulfilling manner.

*"It all started with a vision—a vision of what could be. A shared vision that motivated other people—our team—to be on board with us."*

— Dr. John Jameson

You, too, can bring your vision to life. You can develop or enhance a workplace that brings joy and fulfillment to yourself and to the other people with whom you work: a workplace that is both enjoyable and profitable.

## THE FOUNDATION OF YOUR VISION: *VALUES*

As you write your vision of your IDEAL PRACTICE, start with your values. John Maxwell says the following about values: "Values are enduring beliefs or ideals that drive one's behavior. It tells us 'what is and what is not good' in our actions. These guiding principles influence how we make our choices, what choices we do make, and often times how we are judged in our actions by these choices."

What are the imperative values that are essential elements of your work and of your organization? Webster defines *value* as "something that is held up as important. A principle or quality intrinsically valuable or desirable." Synonyms for *values* include *standards, morals, ethics, ideals, principles,* and *significance.*

Think about your organization. What is your purpose—why do you exist? What impact do you want to have on others? What legacy are you creating? Think of the values that you believe must be honored in every action, interaction, or decision that you make. These values must infiltrate everything you do that includes money. Otherwise, you risk spending a career totally unfulfilled. A tragic loss.

What values are most important to your team? What values do you all agree upon as imperative? This is a great discussion to have with your team members. These value words will appear in your Mission Statement and are an essential part of your VISION STATEMENT. For example: integrity, honesty, compassion, etc.

# YOUR IMPERATIVE VALUES

1. _____
2. _____
3. _____
4. _____
5. _____

# GOALS: *THE STEPPING STONES OR ACTION PLAN*

Webster defines a *goal* as "the end toward which effort is directed." Goals are the stepping stones that move you toward your IDEAL PRACTICE. Most people have only a vague idea of what they want to achieve in life. However, a few develop that clear vision by writing goals and following a process of goal accomplishment. Just a handful of people invest the time and the energy necessary to plan for the successful achievement of their goals.

> *"Studies show that less than one percent of Americans write down specific goals for themselves each year. That's a shame, because writing down your goals is powerful."*
> — David Bach, *Smart Women Finish Rich: 9 Steps to Achieving Financial Security and Funding Your Dreams*

Write specific goals in these three areas:
1. Spiritual, family, personal

2. Business and career

3. Self improvement

It is just fine to write financial goals as well. Plan for your financial success. That is an essential part of a safe and secure life.

Following this six-step process will lead you toward goal accomplishment:

1. Write the goal. Be clear. Be specific.

2. Design a plan of action. What do you need to do or who do you need to bring this goal to a state of reality?

3. Who will be responsible for each action item?

4. Assign a time frame to each action item and to the final goal. Write both short time lines and final deadlines. Adjust as needed.

5. Evaluate your progress routinely. Don't write your goals, stick them in a forgotten notebook in a drawer, and never look at them. Whether these are personal goals or goals for your practice, continue to review them and evaluate your progress.

6. Celebrate the small victories and the major victories along the way. Dr. Michael Le Boeuf says the greatest management principle in the world is this: "That which is rewarded is repeated." So, don't forget to recognize steps taken toward a goal. Remember to say thank you. Positive reinforcement will always lead to greater performance than negative reinforcement or no recognition at all.

## GOAL ACCOMPLISHMENT

**GOAL:**

| Strategies | Responsible Person | Time Frame | Evaluation |
|---|---|---|---|
| #1 | | | |
| #2 | | | |
| #3 | | | |
| #4 | | | |
| #5 | | | |
| #6 | | | |

**(SUPPLEMENTAL MANUAL: 2.1)**

Your goals can become benchmarks for decisions you are making—both in the business and in your personal life. Each time you make a purchase or invest money, ask yourself if this purchase or investment upholds your values and if it fits with your short-term or long-term goals. (Of course, there will be times when you buy something just for the fun of it.) But, at the end of the month, look at your checkbook or analyze your bills, including credit card bills, and ask yourself these questions: "Did I make purchases this month that made sense, for the most part? Do my purchases support my values and goals?"

If you find that too often you are saying "no" to those questions, consider making some alterations in your purchasing patterns and decisions. Getting yourself into a financial bind by spending more than you make or buying something without evaluating the end results you are seeking can cause your relationship with money to become harmful and truly unrewarding. This in turn can have a negative impact on the other people in your life. Getting yourself into a financial bind can result from not clarifying your goals—the things that are most important to you. Your money may be spent on "things," and you may miss the joy and peace of a fulfilled life. Be careful. Respect the values you hold essential and let your relationship with money support those values.

> *"Time is more valuable than money. You can get more money, but you cannot get more time."*
>
> — Jim Rohn

## THE MIRROR EFFECT

In the world of business—and you are in business—your dynamic with money can be positive and healthy or it can be negative and stress-filled. If your practice—your business—is financially sound and you and your team are secure and happy, you will attract people who are the same. Put up a mirror in front of the face of your practice and know that the patients and the relationships you have with your patients will be a direct reflection of what you are putting out into the world. If you are stressed about money, driven by money, don't have enough money to pay the bills, or don't feel equitably compensated for your work, those negative feelings will be projected, and you will attract people who are negative, demanding, and dominating, or who don't have enough money of their own! The mirror effect. And not being financially stable can have an impact—sometimes harmful—on decisions you make.

I'm going to ask you once again to think honestly about your relationship with money for a few minutes. Your attitude toward and relationship with money can have a positive or negative effect on other team members and patients.

For example, if the financial coordinator is not comfortable with money or can't imagine investing money over a certain amount on dental care, people will pick up on that hesitation—immediately. No matter how great the coordinator's verbal skills, that discomfort may have an adverse impact on the patient's decision to proceed with treatment and the financial responsibility.

I have had the privilege of working with a fantastic treatment coordinator from New York City, Sophia Dunkley of S and D Consulting, for quite some time. She says, "I start each day thinking 'I am here to help you—to serve you. If you are willing and if you want this treatment, we will find a solution that is just right for you.'"

The goal of the treatment coordinator or financial coordinator is to "find a financial solution for each patient." Remember that a person would not be in your office if they did not want or need something. The American Dental Association's nationwide surveys state that the number one thing that prevents people from coming to the dentist is money. None of us are surprised by that, but this is not a barrier to avoid. Rather, this helps to define the importance of studying financing, including what options to make available, how to present them, and how to overcome objections. These are not skills that are magically absorbed. These are skills that must be studied, practiced, and applied.

And, before we dive into the nitty-gritty of financing, let's pause one moment to reflect on one of the most important personal attributes that will nurture your relationships with your team, patients, family, friends—and your own self: gratitude.

## WHAT IS GRATITUDE?

Webster defines *gratitude* as "a feeling of thankfulness and appreciation." Studies show a person's well-being and ultimate happiness can be improved by nurturing and developing a state of gratitude. By expressing your appreciation to and for others, studies reveal increased energy, optimism, and empathy.

Mentally strong people don't waste time feeling sorry for themselves. Healthy people exchange self-pity for gratitude. They learn from problems and challenges and gain strength. Dr. Joe Dispenza says that when we take the negative emotion out of an experience, on the other side we discover wisdom. My personal coach, Alan Cohen, states the following, "Gratitude is not a result of things that happen to us; it is an attitude we cultivate by practice. The more we are thankful for, the more we will find to be thankful for. The universe always gives you more of what you are focusing on."

# Be Grateful

### By Cathy Jameson

*Be grateful for this day—it is full of joy.*

*Awaken yourself to its opportunity.*

*Be grateful for your health—it is a blessing often taken for granted.*

*Make effort to preserve it.*

*Be grateful for your many talents.*

*They often rest under the "bushel basket"—untapped.*

*Seek to discover and develop your gifts.*

*Be grateful for your beloved friends—those who are there when you need them.*

*Be grateful for your family—those who love you unconditionally.*

*When it's all said and done, they will be beside you.*

*Be grateful for your work—your chosen career.*

*There lies your opportunity to give back, to make a difference, to pursue a purpose.*

*Be grateful for your challenges—the traumas of life.*

*These mountains develop your strength, your courage, your wisdom.*

*Be grateful for your mind—the director of your being.*

*Direct your mind with clarity of focus. Your actions will follow proportionately.*

*Believe it—and it shall be.*

*Be grateful for God—the Highest of Powers.*

*Call on Him for direction, guidance, strength and energy.*

*Your requests will be heard. Your expressions of gratitude will be valued.*

*Be grateful for this day.*

*Be able to look back on it and say, "I'm glad I did…"*

*Rather than saying, "I wish I had…"*

*Be grateful.*

*The joy and opportunity are there.*

*You must open yourself up in order to see it—and receive it.*

*Be grateful for your ability to do just that!*

*Be grateful.*

Be grateful for what you have or for your ability to foresee wonderful things in the future. Believe in possibilities. Start by writing the vision of your ideal life. Express gratitude for the things you've learned—even the difficult lessons. On the other side of difficulties are insights for a bright future.

## COLLECTING IDEAS

1. Go to a quiet place and think about what you would like your ideal business to be like—or your ideal job, or life. Take a notebook and pen with you to take notes.

2. Think about and answer the questions in this chapter.

3. Acknowledge and feel grateful for the good things in your life.

4. Identify places where practice improvement can take place—places where the work environment could be healthier for you and for your teammates.

5. Write goals, the heart of strategic planning. The "how do we make that happen" part! Follow the 6-step action plan outlined in this chapter.

# CHAPTER THREE

# FINANCIAL OPTIONS FOR YOU AND YOUR PATIENTS

*"Offer a patient the best dental care possible. Make the financing of the dentistry comfortable and affordable. Then, get out of the way and let the patient have a chance to say 'yes' to the very best."*

— Dr. John Jameson

The financial options I have recommended throughout my career have two major goals: (1) to help more people receive needed and/or desired care, and (2) to help more dentists perform the kind of dentistry they want to provide *in the way* they want to provide it. This makes for happy patients and happy dental professionals.

At Jameson Management, we have served over 2,500 clients and consulted in every state and in 31 countries. These are the options we have placed in all of these practices, whether large or small, new or established, urban or rural, solo or group, mid-level, Dental Service Organization (DSO), or corporate. The options that I recommend offer flexibility as well as firmness. They will meet the needs of most of your patients. In addition, consistently following this program will get you out of the banking business and will let you concentrate on what you do best: practice dentistry.

Additional benefits:

- Lower cost of operation in the area of financial management

- Less time spent on statements and collection by your team members

- Greater cash flow

- Greater treatment acceptance
- Enhanced scheduling

# MODEL OF SUCCESS

Here is what I call the "Model of Success." It is the standard by which all of your systems can be set up, administered, and monitored. While this may sound strange at first, think it through. It makes sense for a productive, profitable dental practice:

1. See fewer patients in a day.

2. Provide as much treatment as possible at each appointment— when and where that is appropriate for the patient and you.

3. See the patient for fewer visits.

4. Minimize the number of team members because you will be more organized.

5. Maximize the talent of your team members.

6. Increase the profit margin of the practice.

7. Share the profit with the team members and doctors.

8. Reduce stress.

Sound Good? Read on.

### ▶ Option #1. A 5% Accounting or Fee Reduction for Payment in Full—Before Treatment is Rendered

For those patients who have healthy savings or checking accounts, this option gives them an incentive to pay in advance. This option is for cash or check. Anyone who has ever been responsible for scheduling knows that if a patient pays for the treatment in advance, they will show up for those appointments. Reducing no shows and broken appointments will reduce stress and add to your bottom line.

Offer this option for cases of a certain amount or more. The amount where this option begins is up to you. Have a discussion with your business team. Ask them where most people begin having trouble writing a check. They will know. In our practice, we offer this option for cases of $500 or more. We practice in a small rural area where our wonderful patients are *salt of the earth people* who live on budgets. For most of our patients, an investment of $500 or more is significant. That being said, this can be different for every practice. Wherever you decide to begin offering this option—offer it to everyone.

How do you present this option?

**Financial Coordinator (FC):** *Ms. Jones, many of our patients have chosen to have their fee reduced. Would that be of interest to you?*

Or, more simply,

**FC:** *Ms. Jones, we do offer a payment option that would reduce your fee. Would you be interested in hearing about this?*

Or, even more simply,

**FC:** *Ms. Jones, would you be interested in having your fee reduced?*

**Ms. Jones:** *Of course. How do I do that?*

**FC:** *If you pay for your treatment before the doctor begins, we will reduce your fee by 5%. If we aren't involved with the bookkeeping, that saves us both time and money, and we would like to pass those savings on to you.*

Be totally prepared before you discuss finances. Know the total fee for the complete treatment plan and be prepared to present the entire plan and entire fee. Be prepared to offer all of the options, because your goal is to find the option that works best for the patient—one that you have already determined works for you. Know how much the 5% fee reduction (or you may choose to say "cash courtesy") would be for the patient and present this in a positive manner. Be sure to always stress the benefits to the patient. That's what they are interested in—how something will benefit them.

### Example

Let's say that the patient has a $3,000 treatment plan.

**FC:** *Ms. Jones, we would be more than happy to reduce your fee. If you pay for your treatment in full before the doctor begins, we will reduce your fee by 5%. That would be a savings of $150. That's a significant amount of savings, and I wanted to be sure to offer that to you. Would that work for you?*

You will be pleasantly surprised at how many patients are glad to receive an incentive for full payment. Listen well. Determine needs. Present the dentistry in terms of *their* needs. Stress the benefits of treatment—the end results. Establish a solid, trusting relationship. Do these things and your patients will be much more likely to accept treatment. If they agree to proceed, offer the fee reduction as an option. Many people will accept. You are dollars ahead to offer this reduction versus carrying any accounts on your own books.

### ▶ Option #2. Half of the Total Fee to Reserve the Appointment and the Other Half at the Time of the First Appointment

Historically, most practices have offered half at the preparation and half at the insertion for prosthetic appointments. There have been some difficulties with the following:

1. Patients reserve long appointments but then don't show up or cancel at the last minute. This can cause hesitation to schedule long appointments for fear of large voids in the schedule.

2. Patients make the first payment at the prep appointment, but fail to pay the balance at the insertion. "Oh, I'm sorry. I forgot my checkbook!" Now you have additional accounts receivable. Certainly you could ask for a credit card payment or send a statement and a self-addressed envelope and ask for an immediate turnaround on the balance—but does this always happen? NO!

3. At the time of insertion, the patient knows he doesn't have the money for the final payment, so he doesn't show up.

As we all know, when a person cancels at the last minute or just doesn't show up, this is a huge time management problem. It's costly and stressful to all members of the team.

I recommend for your crown and bridge appointments—or for any treatments that involve multiple appointments—you ask for an initial investment of half the total fee when you schedule the first appointment. Then, at the time of the first appointment, collect the second half.

Patients will be fine with this option when this it's presented well. You'll find that most people will comply with what they find is expected in your practice. Consistency is critical.

> **FC:** "*Ms. Jones, we will be reserving two hours of Dr. Jameson's time just for you. He and his clinical assistant want to give you their full, undivided attention. In order for us to reserve this much time, we ask for half of the fee to reserve the appointment and then the final half at the first appointment. This will let you spread the payments out into two equal payments, we will be able to prepare excellently for you, and we'll be able to pay the laboratory expenses so that they can prepare your restorations.*"

This does let a patient spread the payment out a bit—perhaps more than a couple of pay periods. The point of this option is to get the patient's commitment to show up for the appointment. You're committing to reserve a large block of the doctor's time, and it's okay to ask for their commitment in return.

There is such an abundance of broken appointments, no shows, and cancellations in the industry that something different must be done. John Maxwell says, "If you keep on doing what you are doing, you will keep on getting what you are getting." You are running a business. Certainly you want to be gracious and considerate to your patients. However, it is acceptable to ask your patients to respect the importance of your time.

Be sure to collect the second half before the patient receives those preps! When you confirm the appointment, reiterate your financial agreement and ask the patient if he is prepared to pay the second half of the fee at his appointment. If he isn't, then reschedule at a time that is more appropriate. Confirm well enough in advance to make sure things go well—either with the scheduling or with the financing. Most of you are digitally confirming and have a sequence of confirmations. Make sure that as you near the appointment that you are providing a *two day in advance* confirmation, and some practices provide additional confirmations the day of the appointment—even an hour or two before. You need to know what you can count on and alterations that may need to be made.

> **Business Administrator (BA):** *Ms. Jones, this is Cathy with Dr. Jameson's dental office. Dr. Jameson has asked that I call to tell you that he is looking forward to seeing you Wednesday, June 25th at 8:30 in the morning. As you recall, Dr. Jameson has reserved two hours of his time just for you. He's totally prepared for your appointment.*
>
> *Ms. Jones, during our consultation appointment two weeks ago, you made an initial investment of half the total fee, or $1,500. The other half of the fee, or the other $1,500, will be due tomorrow. You have chosen to pay with a credit card. So I'll have everything ready for you. In fact, we can take care of that when you arrive and then we can seat you for your appointment. Again, we look forward to seeing you tomorrow.*

Some people say, "Oh, our patients won't make their full payment until their treatment is finished and are sure that they like it." Really? Well, you stand behind your work, don't you? Hopefully so! And, I hope your patients know they can count on you to make sure everything is right. Let them know that you stand behind your work—whether the financial responsibility has been completed or not.

If you want a more lenient option but one that integrates the initial investment (which offsets no shows and broken appointments), ask for one-third at the reservation, one-third at the preparation, and one-third at the insertion. However, this option still puts you at risk for that insertion appointment, and I am interested in you not being at risk for any payments.

## ▶ Option #3. Payment by the Appointment

In order to offer this financial option, the Business Administrator or Financial Coordinator must have a complete treatment plan from the clinical team. It's impossible to inform a person of his/her financial responsibility per appointment if you are not sure what is going to be provided at each appointment.

The treatment plan must provide complete information. Just saying you are going to do some *fillings* doesn't work. How many teeth? How many surfaces? What type of material? Etc. All of these details are necessary before proper financial discussions can take place.

Please, always do a comprehensive diagnosis, a complete treatment plan, and a fabulous consultation on all cases for all patients. When discussing a treatment plan that involves multiple appointments, and if the person needs to spread payments throughout the course of treatment, do so in the following manner:

1. Determine the total fee.

2. Divide the fee equally into the number of appointments.

3. Collect those equally calculated payments at each appointment.

4. Make sure full payment is accomplished by the end of the treatment.

If you calculate and collect the specific amount due at each particular appointment based on what procedures you are doing at each appointment, you run the risk of the patient falling out of treatment. They may complete only a part of the treatment and then decide they don't want to spend any more money. By dividing the fee into equal payments spread over the course of treatment, you reduce that possibility. In most cases, the patient would have paid a portion of upcoming treatments in advance. Thus, you reduce the risk of the patient falling out of treatment or canceling appointments.

### Example

**BA:** *Ms. Jones, the total investment you will be making for the treatment the doctor has recommended to you is $1,200. How would you like to take care of that?*

(Then, stop and listen. Let the patient take the lead.)

**Ms. Jones:** *Oh, dear! That's so much? I would have to pay this out as I go!*

**BA:** *So, paying for the complete treatment at one time is not a possibility for you. Am I correct?*

**Ms. Jones:** *Yes. There is no way.*

**BA:** *I can certainly appreciate that. But, as you indicated, this is the type of treatment you wish to receive. Correct?*

**Ms. Jones:** *Oh, yes. I know I need to get this done—and I don't want things to get any worse.*

**BA:** *Then, may I introduce some options for you that would allow you to pay less or pay over the course of the treatment?*

**Ms. Jones:** *Yes. Please.*

**BA**: *Let me tell you about the wonderful payment options we have here in our practice.* (Offer Option #1 and/or #2.)

**Ms. Jones:** *No. Those don't work for me. I'd just like to pay as I go.*

**BA:** *That will be just fine. We can do that. The way we handle that is like this. The total investment will be $1,200. The doctor will be seeing you for three appointments. So, we can spread the $1,200 evenly over the three appointments. That would be $400 per appointment. And, he will need approximately two weeks between each appointment, so this allows you to spread the payments out evenly and over the course of a couple of months. By the time you complete your treatment, your financial responsibility will be complete as well.*

**Ms. Jones:** *Now that sounds much better. I can do that.*

### ▶ Option #4. Bankcards

Major bankcards are making significant efforts to capture a larger segment of the healthcare market. They are informing the public that using a bankcard for the financing of dental/medical care makes good sense. These companies can afford to market to the consumer in a large way. Every dental office will be a benefactor of their brilliant marketing efforts.

Surveys by bankcard companies have asked, "Would you use a bankcard to finance your dental care?" Approximately 75% of the respondents said, "Yes." However, only 6% of dentistry in the United States is being financed on a bankcard presently. The next question is asked of dental consumers, "Most of you say that you would use a bankcard to finance your dental care, but only 6% of you are doing so. Why?"

The answers were: (1) "My dentist doesn't accept bankcards" and (2) "I don't know if my dentist accepts bankcards."

Inform your patient family—and the people within your drawing area—of the fact that bankcards are accepted and encouraged in your practice. It can determine whether a family comes to you or not, and whether a person accepts treatment recommendations or not.

You must ask for these cards. Don't just hang up a sign or put a notice on your front desk and think people will respond. You have to mention and encourage the use of this option. In your patient education newsletters, special mailings, social media, your website, newspaper announcements, your statements, and during your financial consultations, encourage people to use this option. Stress the benefits of financing with a bankcard. Don't assume people know you accept bankcards. **Obviously they don't!** Assumption is the lowest form of communication. Don't assume anything!

Consider developing a form that lets a patient give you a signature on file for use of their bankcard. When asked if this was acceptable, VISA said not only was this acceptable, but it was recommended. They have their own credit card authorization forms (SUPPLEMENTAL MANUAL: 3.1), but say it is just fine for dentists to do this themselves.

You can do any of the following things with these authorizations forms:

a. **Place any balance after insurance pays on their credit card up to a certain amount. Or, put the full balance for treatment on the credit card if insurance doesn't pay for any reason.** If you are accepting insurance on assignment, you do your very best to estimate the amount the insurance program will pay, and you collect the co-pay at the time of the service. However, from time to time, the insurance company may not pay what you estimate. Thus, there will be a remaining balance due from the patient. This is tough money to collect. You run the risk of the patient becoming disgruntled with you—not the insurance company! You run the risk of the patient delaying payment—which reduces the bottom-line profit of the treatment. And/or you run the risk of the patient not paying at all, turning the balance due into a source of conflict with you: "the fee was too high", "the treatment didn't need to be done", "a lower fee service could have been provided", "you didn't figure things correctly", and so on. All inaccurate and untrue statements—but not in the mind of the patient.

b. **Place one—or a series—of regular payments on the credit card.** With the patient, determine the amount, date, and length of time that payments will be placed on their credit card. This is a good option for any past-due accounts you may have lingering as accounts receivable. If the patient needs time to pay, this can be an option.

Don't forget you can accept a credit card payment over the phone, also. Even if you don't have a preauthorization, you can call a patient and make a payment with the patient's verbal authorization. Then, send a copy of the receipt to the patient. This is appropriate for balances after insurance pays and for past-due accounts.

Soon—once you learn to *COLLECT WHAT YOU PRODUCE*—you won't have any accounts receivable. But if you have accounts receivable right now and are sending statements, be sure to choose a billing statement format that allows for a bankcard payment: the account number, cardholder's name, expiration date, amount of payment (hopefully the entire amount due!), and the signature. Make it easy for people to pay you! (SUPPLEMENTAL MANUAL: 3.2)

**All visits occurring during a certain period of time can be authorized for the patient's credit card.** This is great for families who may be sending different members of the family to the office at various times, or for people with recurring visits, such as orthodontics or periodontal therapy, etc.

Offer all major bankcards: VISA, Mastercard, Discover, and American Express.

The service fee for all the programs is about the same. American Express may be a bit higher. (But you WANT those American Express cardholders as patients!) Depending on how much bankcard usage you do in your practice, you may be able to negotiate lower service fees with your bank. In addition, if you are a member of the ADA, very reasonable rates are accessible.

The minimal amount of service fee you pay for bankcard usage is far less of a cost than carrying the account on your own books or losing the case. Don't worry about the service charge. Running your own credit business is financially devastating and inadequate at best.

### ▶ Option #5. Patient/Healthcare Financing Programs

John was the 18th doctor in the world to accept patient financing in his practice. He became involved with the first patient financing company not long after a wonderful dentist, Dr. T. Warren Center, founded that company—then called Dent-A Med. (A bit of a history lesson, right there!) Upon hearing of this new company, we immediately invited the company representative who was actually a VP, to come to our office for a noon team meeting. (Remember—we were in the middle of the oil crisis.) We signed up immediately and by 5:00 that afternoon, we had already signed up three people for over $5,000 of total treatment. Fees were much lower than they are now. That was a great deal of dentistry!

"People kept telling me that they couldn't afford the care I was recommending. They knew they needed the treatment. They could see it on the photographs I was taking. But the economy was suffering and people were unsure and cautious. They would want me to just "patch them up" until the economy straightened out. Well, starting with the first patient after our luncheon team meeting, I asked the patients, 'If I told you that for $35-$50 per month we could fix this tooth correctly with a long-lasting, stable restoration, would that make it possible for us to go ahead?' And

patient after patient said yes. We signed up three people that afternoon and scheduled over $5,000 worth of dentistry. And that was in one afternoon! That happened every day after that. Because of patient financing programs, we were able to provide millions of dollars of dentistry throughout time."
— Dr. John Jameson

Use of these programs gets you, the dentist, out of the banking business while still allowing patients the opportunity to spread the payment of treatment over several months. Monthly payments can support the financial situation of the majority of families.

Do not think that financial assistance is not needed in your practice—or in any practice. A recent study performed by the ADA asked the question, "If you needed to make a one-time dental purchase of $500, could you?" Approximately 77% of the American population said that they could not afford a one time *out-of-pocket* dental purchase of $500 unless they had a way to pay it out over time.

You and I both know that $500 can't even buy a crown—let alone a root canal, post and core, and a crown. Most people live on budgets and care more about the monthly payments than the total investment. If they want the treatment and see the benefit of the treatment, they will be more likely to proceed if they spread the payment out over time.

According to a 2019 Federal Reserve Survey, four out of ten Americans can't cover a $400 emergency in their home or lives, including a dental emergency or dental need, without financial assistance or without selling some of their possessions.

A patient financing system does the following:

1.  Provides financial assistance for healthcare, including dentistry. It is not a service that is in competition with other bankcards. It is not in competition with food, entertainment, clothes, or vacations, etc. This type of program allows families and individuals to establish a line of credit for healthcare. What a great idea!

2.  Offers lower payments. People can receive needed or desired care, the best available, but make small monthly payments and spread those payments out over a comfortable length of time, determined by how much they can afford per month. Thus, the total investment does not become such an enormous barrier. A comfortable monthly payment becomes the solution.

3.  Provides convenience. People can apply in your office.

4.  Works in conjunction with insurance. If a patient has dental insurance but cannot afford the co-pay, the patient can finance the co-pay. More people who have dental insurance will use it because their private pay portion isn't a barrier.

5.  Improves your collections with same day payment, insurance co-pays, balances after insurance pays, and, most of all a much higher case acceptance rate. And, of course you need to produce in order to collect!

## TYPES OF PATIENT FINANCING OPTIONS

1.  **A revolving payment plan.** With this option, a family establishes a line of credit with the financing company. All members of the family can participate. The family is required to pay a minimum

payment per month just like bankcards. The minimum payment is usually about 3% of the outstanding balance. So, for $1,000 worth of dental care, if a patient or family can afford $30 per month, they can receive treatment. I think we will all agree that *MOST* families can afford $30 per month.

The line of credit belongs to the family. If they use the credit line that means less credit is available. However, as they make monthly payments, that credit is opened up again. If a family maxes out their limit but finds they need some additional care, the patient can request an expanded line of credit. If the family wants to pay the account off early or make higher payments than is required, that is just fine. There is no penalty for prepayment.

2. **Deferred Interest Plans.** For shorter term financing needs, such as six, twelve, eighteen, or twenty-four months, no interest is charged on purchases of $200 or more. A minimum monthly payment is required and the patient needs to pay the full amount due by the end of the time frame selected. If "life happens" and the patient cannot complete the payment agreement, the interest that would have accrued on the account is charged from the original date of the agreement.

This is a great option. People love this! Determine how much per month is comfortable for the patient. See how long the agreement needs to be in order for that desired monthly payment to be possible. The patient has a "safety net." If for any reason they are unable to complete the total agreement amount by the pre-determined length of that agreement, the interest that would have accrued will be placed onto their remaining balance and the monthly payments will continue. They will not be turned over for collection, nor will any negative information be placed on their credit history as long as they continue to pay under the auspices of the revised agreement.

Don't present this as a negative. Do a great job of making the financial agreement in the first place and present this as a benefit. A safety net.

Doctors, you may pay a higher service fee for this option than for others. Well, sing all the way to the bank! If you were to carry the account, it would cost you much more. Or if the patient does not find a comfortable financial option, that person will walk out your door saying, "Gee Doc, I just can't afford this. I'll just have to think about it." GET THE AGREEMENT. THEN YOU CAN DO THE DENTISTRY.

This option has been available for quite some time now and is popular with patients for the obvious reason of the interest free aspect. The various financing companies have different ways of offering this option to your patients. Offer all lengths that are available. Don't "cut your nose off to spite your face" due to the service fees you will pay. You cannot afford to carry the accounts yourself and you cannot afford to lose that patient.

3. **Extended Payment Plans.** Most patient financing companies offer an extended payment option: twenty-four, thirty-six, forty-eight, or sixty-month periods with reduced APR and fixed monthly payments required until paid in full. The amount of APR and the amount of the monthly payment is determined by both the size of the line of credit and the length of time desired. These extended payment plans are great for your large and comprehensive restorative, implant, and/or cosmetic cases.

## PATIENT EDUCATION

Excellent patient educational materials and support data are provided to you from the individual companies, but it is up to you to use them and to spread the word constantly. Don't think that just because you've spoken to a patient once, or sent out patient educational material once, that this is enough. The rule of thumb about marketing is that you never stop spreading the message. Few people "get it" immediately. Repetition is the key to learning. Plus, someone may not have had the need the first time they "heard" about patient financing, but life may have changed, and they need it now. Keep presenting. Do not give up. Consider the following key recommendations:

1. Study the various companies and get involved with the one or ones you believe will work for you.

2. Take as much time as necessary to train on how to administer and present the program.

3. Don't sign up and then put the materials in a drawer. Offer the program to everyone. People who buy a Mercedes Benz often buy one because they can afford the monthly payments. Top quality dentistry is the same. People want the best. They just need a way to pay for it. Usually they don't pay for the car in full and then drive it off the lot!

## What if the patient doesn't get accepted?

So, you say, "Terrific." But what if the patient doesn't get accepted, then what? Some offices have a healthcare financing program but become discouraged because they see the benefit of the program, recommend it, get people to fill out the applications, then the patients are denied. Sometimes these offices get so discouraged with the programs that they are afraid to present this option at all.

There may be several reasons why a program may not have worked well for you in the past. Please consider looking at these programs with a new light and a new level of encouragement. Without a strong financial program that includes third-party financing, you will stifle your growth, productivity, and enjoyment.

The key to the success of your program is how well you manage the program. Period. The programs work and work well. It doesn't matter what part of the country you live in or how large your city or town may be. We have seen these financing programs make a 10–40% difference in a practice's revenue stream. What matters is how well the practice promotes and administers the program.

Don't offer your program a couple of times, have patients
turned down for a line of credit, and then never offer it
again—with you deciding that "it doesn't work." These
programs work. Most practices don't work the program.
Keep offering it. The law of averages will work in your favor.
How well you present this option and overcome objections
will make all the difference.

Schedule training for the entire team with your company of choice. Once training has been completed, hold a team meeting and practice the verbal skills of presenting the program and overcoming objections patients may present. Study "Ways to Maximize a Healthcare Financing Program" outlined in this book and implement these strategies.

However, no matter how well you administer the system into your practice, not every patient will get accepted. The company will be doing a very careful credit screening of the patient. These professionals will help you to make good business decisions about financing your dentistry. If a patient is not granted a line of credit by a professional financing company, do we want to make a loan to this patient?

Probably not. Rather, you may need to back off the treatment plan just a bit and provide treatment based on the patient's ability to pay as they go or payment by the appointment. You want to do as much dentistry as possible without financially stressing the patient or yourself.

If a patient does not qualify for a line of credit, ask him/her if a family member would co-sign. I cannot tell you how many of our patients were able to get a line of credit because a family member or a close friend was willing to co-sign. Sometimes people have a financial predicament (such as divorce) that puts a black mark on their credit score. Give people a chance to get healthy and to reestablish a good credit rating. Don't give up too soon.

Another way to deal with the patient who is not granted a line of credit is to do *layaway dentistry*. This means that the patient makes monthly payments to you. You place these payments in an account as a growing *credit*. Then, when he/she has the money saved, you can proceed with the dentistry.

Many times we do "just because" dentistry. John provides care for a person just because. He would rather provide free care as a chosen love gift instead of making an unrealistic financial arrangement with a person only to be disappointed or to be placed in a situation of dealing with an uncollectable account.

In certain situations, we refer patients to the dental school for care by students. These students will, of course, provide excellent care. This is an excellent service to both the indigent family and to the students.

> If a patient doesn't receive a line of credit from your healthcare financing program, address that issue in the following way:
>
> **BA:** *Ms. Jones, the financial program with whom we work has let us know that at this time they are not able to extend a line of credit to you. You may certainly contact the company to discuss this. We encourage you to do so. Many times there is incorrect information on a credit report and this would give you a chance to update your report. However, for now, let's discuss other financial possibilities that will let you proceed with the care Dr. Jameson has recommended.*

Do not use the terms *approved* or *not approved* with your patients. These are demeaning phrases and can cause major embarrassment. Embarrassment is a primary emotion which when stimulated can appear as anger. Be careful with how you handle this issue.

### ▶ Option #6. Banking and Lending Institutions

Historically, banks and other types of lending institutions were not generous with their *loans* for dentistry. However, over the last decade, there has been more acceptance of health-oriented loans from banks and other lending institutions. In fact, major lending entities who have been solid in other industries have entered the dental profession in a major way. And, they are loaning BIG amounts to credit-worthy patients.

These companies are not just in the healthcare business, but they know that healthcare can be a boom to their organizations. Also, they like *getting in good* with the patients so that when they need money for other kinds of loans, they might consider their company.

### ▶ Option #7. Insurance Management

This is not a book about dental insurance. I highly recommend the books by Dr. Charles Blair on coding and on insurance administration. In my opinion, Dr. Blair's books are a must for any practice accepting insurance. It is my hope that you will consider the following:

**Be insurance aware, but do not be insurance driven.**

Certainly, dental insurance has been an asset to the profession and to many people who could not or would not receive dental treatment if they did not have dental insurance. However, we all know that insurance is not a pay-all, but is a supplement to healthcare.

You are not required to file insurance for a patient. If you do so, you do so as a service to your patient. The contract is between the patient and the insurance company. For the few private indemnity insurance plans remaining in the world, if a patient has dental insurance, you would collect the entire fee, file the claim for the patient, electronically is preferred, and let the insurance company reimburse the patient directly. The patient can use any of the previously mentioned options for paying for treatment and will receive a reimbursement check quickly—probably more quickly than you would!

If you choose to accept assignment of benefits of insurance claims, collect the expected co-pay or estimated patient's portion at the time of service, file the claim, and then manage the insurance aspect of your practice with care and consistency.

If you are contracted with any managed care programs, including PPO's (preferred provider organizations), you must follow the guidelines outlined by the contract you signed.

### ▶ Option #8. Electronic Funds Transfer

About 97% of electronic funds transfer (EFT) payments clear. The patient completes the necessary paperwork, and together you agree upon the date and amount of the withdrawal, as well as the designated amount. The data is given to the appropriate bank. Then, withdrawals begin.

People are familiar with this type of payment option. Many home mortgage, car, and savings plan programs use a withdrawal system. Certainly, specific criteria must be in place. But, for the most part, everyone has a checking account and can place a withdrawal program into effect. If a withdrawal does not clear, the bank will put it through again. Any charges will be filed against the patient.

## What if financial assistance is needed during an emergency?

If a person comes to your practice in an emergency situation, use the following protocols:

- Determine, as a team, what is truly an emergency situation when the patient needs to be seen that day. Gather information about the patient. Then, if the patient does have an emergency situation, see the person that day. (SUPPLEMENTAL MANUAL: 3.3)

- If this is a new patient, let the patient know that he will be expected to pay the fee for the emergency visit at the time of the service. This is one of the only times to quote a fee over the phone. But, the patient does need to know the fee and expect to pay the fee that day. Even if he has insurance, collect the fee, give him the necessary paperwork, and let him file his own insurance. Then you can gather necessary data about the insurance plan, do a verification of insurance coverage, and file his insurance at the next appointment, if you choose.

- Let the patient know that if the dentist needs to provide treatment, there will be a financial discussion before any treatment is rendered, and that there will not be any financial surprises.

- If the person indicates a concern about finances, inform her/him of your financial options. If the patient is uncomfortable with cash payments and does not have a bankcard, introduce your healthcare financing program. Ask the patient to come in earlier than the scheduled time to complete an application. Then, while the patient is waiting to be seated, or certainly before the dentist renders any treatment beyond emergency care, process the application online. You will know whether or not she has been extended a line of credit and, if so, for how much.

This is valuable information. You do not know this person. Don't make a loan to a stranger! However, you do want to provide the necessary care. By establishing a line of credit with your financing company, both of these needs are fulfilled—they receive needed care, and you receive reimbursement. In addition, you can direct the patient to your website where you, hopefully, have a place for patients to complete an application for your patient financing program. Once their line of credit is established, both you and the patient will be informed.

- If the patient comes in for the emergency visit and the dentist diagnoses necessary treatment and wants to go ahead with that treatment while the patient is there, the following two things must be in place:

  1. You must have time to render treatment without a negative effect on your regularly scheduled patients. If you do not have the time, diagnose, prescribe treatment, get the patient comfortable, and reschedule for the necessary length of time. A trauma case would be an exception. Otherwise, you need to respect the time of your regularly scheduled patients. Palliative treatment only.

  2. Inform the patient of the financial responsibility before treatment is rendered. Patients want to know how much something costs before it is done. In addition, you run the risk of acquiring a bad debt if you don't handle the financial and clinical aspect of an emergency visit with care.

If the patient is in the chair and you diagnose necessary treatment, check to see if you do have time to provide that treatment. If you do, have the business administrator step back to the clinical area to discuss the fee and the options for payment. If the patient needs financial assistance, get an application for your financial program, help her to complete the application, then, digitally send the information to the company. You will know in a matter of minutes whether or not the patient has been extended that line of credit and for how much. Then, let the dentist know that she/he can go ahead with the treatment or if there need another alternative needs to be considered.

This only takes a few minutes and can make a big difference in your financial security. If you analyze your accounts receivable carefully, you may find that a significant portion of those accounts may be emergency patients who never had a firm financial agreement and who never paid.

# CHAPTER FOUR

# GET OUT OF THE BANKING BUSINESS: BECOME MORE *PROFITABLE*

*"If you want something you've never had, you'll have to do something you've never done."*

**— Dave Ramsey, Author of *Financial Peace***

U nderstanding the credit business as it applies to dentistry will help you make the following decisions:

- Get out of the banking business and don't look back.

- Reduce the amount of money spent on the statement and collection portion of your practice.

- Get involved with a healthcare financing program as soon as possible!

- Be more confident in presenting comprehensive dentistry to your patients.

- Build your practice without increasing the overhead related to financial management.

- Learn to communicate financially with confidence and competence.

# COST OF CREDIT

The "credit" portion of your practice refers to patients who have received dental treatment but owe money for those services. They have not paid in full, and you're carrying their balance. This is called "Accounts Receivable." The American Dental Association says that 20% of all accounts receivable in a dental practice are, in fact, uncollected.

In the next few pages, I'm going to show you how much it costs to carry accounts on your own books. You may think that the service fee paid to a patient financing company is high. Wrong! It costs substantially less than if you were to make the loan with your own money and try to collect the balance.

Each practice has its own production figures, so a generalized illustration is imperative. However, the percentages that are included in the following calculations are relevant to every practice. Apply these percentages to your own practice. Run your own numbers. These are accurate and supported by financial experts and the American Dental Association.

# SAMPLE PRACTICE

The accompanying illustration represents a practice that is producing $740,000 per year, which, according to the 2019 surveys from the American Dental Association (ADA), is what the average U.S. general practice is generating. Specialty practices are approximately $400,000 higher.

According to the ADA, the average dental practice receives approximately 50% of its revenue from insurance. If a dental practice has a potential gross annual revenue of $740,000, that would mean approximately $370,000 of that practice's revenue comes from insurance reimbursement. If a practice is heavily involved in PPO's, then this percentage will likely be higher. Revenue means Collections—money in the bank. These collected monies represent actual collections whether from Usual and Customary fees or fees collected from insurance companies. If you are engaged in any managed care programs of any type, including PPO's, your ultimate collections will be the monies you collect after agreed upon adjustments.

About 30% of the income for most dental practices comes from cash, check, or bankcards. For a $740,000 practice, that means about $222,000 comes from cash, checks, or bankcards.

The remaining 20% is the credit portion. Those are the people who are making payments to the practice, and you are sending statements and doing your own collections with these accounts. This is your private pay accounts receivable. For a solo practitioner whose annual collections are $740,000, this represents approximately $148,000 revenue coming in the form of "credit." (Figure 4.1)

## Dental Practice Income by Source

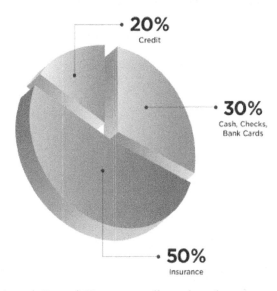

**20%**
Credit

**30%**
Cash, Checks, Bank Cards

**50%**
Insurance

The ADA and *Dental Economics* tell us that the average practice in the U.S. collects approximately 96%. This means that the average dental practice is writing off about 4% or suffers a 4% loss. You may think that is not too bad—96% collection or a 4% loss. Well, let's take a look at that.

| | Value Analysis Example |
|---|---|
| Annual Gross Revenue | $740,000 |
| Insurance (50%) | $370,000 |
| Cash & major credit cards (30%) | $222,000 |
| | |
| Billed Charges (20%) | $148,000 |
| Uncollected Revenue — % of Gross | 4% |
| % of Billed Charges | 20% |
| | |
| Statements Per Month | 250 |
| | |
| Average American Dental Practice Collects | 96% |

© Dr. T. Warren Center

**(Figure 4.1)**

Go back to that average $740,000 practice that is experiencing a 4% write off. Four percent of $740,000 is $29,600—$29,600 not collected! Now answer these questions:

- Did the loss come from the $370,000 that was insurance? I doubt it. You may have a little bit of difficulty getting a quick turnaround on insurance, but you do receive payment.

- Does the 4% loss come from the portion of the practice that is cash across the counter? Probably not. You may have a check bounce every once in a while, but that is not going to have a strong effect on your percentages.

The loss comes from the credit portion of your practice. People may not intend to become past due with their accounts. A patient may say, "I'll pay you $100 a month." Then that becomes difficult for them and they begin to pay $50 a month. Then something happens and that becomes $20 a month. Then they may miss a month or two and the account you thought was going to be a three-month account, is now a six, nine, twelve-month account, or you don't collect it at all. Please note: once you accept a payment, even if it is less than the amount you agreed upon in your financial arrangement, this payment becomes acceptable and is the "norm." So, technically what you should do is return the check and tell the patient that this is the incorrect amount and ask for the agreed upon payment. I know. This is difficult. You have the check in hand and it is hard to return. However, know that if you deposit the check then you have just agreed that this amount is acceptable.

The following graphs outline and illustrate how a family pays their bills once they receive their check or checks each month. Note that healthcare (including dental care) is not listed, but credit cards are high on the list. Also, in the second graph, note the numerous reasons why people use credit cards.

# DIRECT COST OF BILLING AND COLLECTING

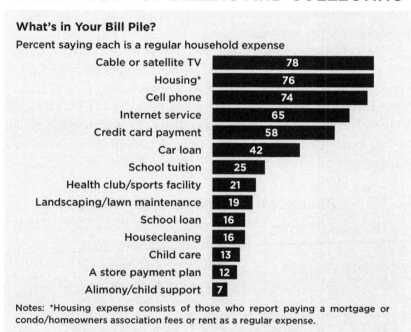

**What's in Your Bill Pile?**
Percent saying each is a regular household expense

| | |
|---|---|
| Cable or satellite TV | 78 |
| Housing* | 76 |
| Cell phone | 74 |
| Internet service | 65 |
| Credit card payment | 58 |
| Car loan | 42 |
| School tuition | 25 |
| Health club/sports facility | 21 |
| Landscaping/lawn maintenance | 19 |
| School loan | 16 |
| Housecleaning | 16 |
| Child care | 13 |
| A store payment plan | 12 |
| Alimony/child support | 7 |

Notes: *Housing expense consists of those who report paying a mortgage or condo/homeowners association fees or rent as a regular expense.

*Source: Pew Research Center*

**Reasons for Credit Card Use**
Percent saying each is a reason they use credit cards

| | |
|---|---|
| More convenient | 66 |
| Pay for unexpected expenses | 60 |
| Finance major purchases | 37 |
| Earn points in reward programs | 33 |
| Pay for things when out of money | 30 |

Notes: *Based on 1,222 respondents who have a credit card payment as a regular expense.

*Source: Pew Research Center*

Let's see how much it costs to run a credit business within your own practice. If you are sending an average of 250 statements a month (which is what the ADA says happens in an average dental practice), you're going to be investing approximately $2,010/year in materials alone—stamps, envelopes, statements, computer materials, etc.

If you send 250 statements a month and you are paying a person $30.00 an hour (national average for a business administrator according to ZipRecruiter and, of course, this varies per state) to handle accounts and if this person is spending about ten minutes per month on each account, you are investing approximately $15,120 per year in the labor costs of managing accounts receivable.

There will be the need for collection calls with certain accounts. Based on a very conservative $40 a month for long distance calls and telephone expenses, that is $480 per year in telephone expense.

Adding these costs together, the cost of billing and collecting for this $740,000 practice is $17,610 minimally. That's 11.8% of the credit portion of this practice. No matter what the total gross production for your practice, these percentages remain the same.

## Direct Cost of Billing and Collecting

| | |
|---|---|
| Materials & Postage | $2,010.00/year (statements and envelopes = $42.50 per month/$510.00 per year. Postage at $.50 per stamp = $137.50 per month/$1,650 per year. |
| Labor | $15,120: reviewing accounts, running statements, stuffing envelopes, stamping, mailing. Collection calls. (based on 2019 ZipRecruiter National Average Salary for a Business Administrator) |
| Long Distance Calls/ Phone Expense | $480/year |
| **Total** | **$17,610** **11.8% of Billed Charges** |

© Dr. T. Warren Center

While this is an extraordinary expense, most offices are sending statements digitally. This is, of course, much more cost efficient. You will still have the labor costs of a person reviewing the account to make sure everything is accurate, and preparing the computer to send statements appropriately. Certainly, the computer takes a big strain off of the historical task of sending statements.

However, look at this report from Consumer Action indicating that not everyone wants to transition to electronic statements.

**"In a recent online survey conducted by Consumer Action, the vast majority of respondents noted that they prefer to receive all types of bills by mail—even when they opt to pay the bill online. Depending on the account category, 45-74 percent of respondents said that they choose paper over electronic notifications for insurance, utilities, medical, mortgages, credit cards and property taxes." I was surprised by this—are you?**

It interests me to see that such a large percentage of consumers want their medical information to come to them in a regular paper statement. Perhaps it would be good consumer/customer service to ask those who have an account with you how they prefer to receive their statement. (Hopefully, you will work your way right out of doing any statements at all!)

Of course, when you provide electronic billing, your patients receive an email that alerts them of their option to pay online using a credit or debit card with an automatic bill payment. You would receive authorization from the patient to receive payment/funds from their bank account.

**Business Administrators, you must be exceptionally well organized and carefully alert yourself of important notes regarding payments in your electronic files.**

But, like we just read, most consumers prefer paper statements particularly for financial and medical matters, according to Consumer Action (CA). CA says the following, "Patients value having a hard copy record of what they owe or what they've paid. Paper statements help some people remember to pay their bills on time, provide proof when disputing an error, and serve as a simple system for record keeping."

Certain "mature" folks, are not digitally savvy or don't even own a computer. About 1/3 of people in America do not have adequate access to the Internet (Pew Research, 2019).

If you are filing insurance, be sure to enter any insurance payments the day that payment arrives. If there is any balance that insurance does not cover, send a statement to the patient that very day. Do not wait for a pre-determined billing date or billing cycle. The ability to collect that balance will be increased if you send the statement immediately.

Some insurance companies are providing electronic funds transfer directly into the doctor's account. Thus, checks from the insurance company would not come directly to the practice, but would be a direct deposit into the bank. The business administrator must be sure to keep track of these payments. Most software programs make this possible. If your software does not have an option for electronic funds transfer, then set up a separate payment type for these payments such as AETNA EFT PAYMENT. Again, the critical factor is to keep careful track of these deposits. It is absolutely essential that you make sure you are being paid equitably and appropriately by each insurance company and you will not know this unless you track it! Balance each payment so that you will know if you are managing each patient's account accurately. Remember that the majority of the money coming into a dental practice is coming in the form of insurance checks. TRACK THIS! In fact, you may need to hold a discussion with your bank to determine exactly how you will be notified of any and all EFT deposits or payments.

## Receivables Management Cost

In addition to the $29,600 in write-offs or uncollectibles, there is one more cost that goes along with managing accounts receivable. The world of banking tells us that for every month that an account sits on your own books doing nothing for you, it loses approximately .83% of its worth or a 10% loss over the year. This is called **"the loss of the dollar."** If you have an average total collection of $148,000 per year in accounts receivable or billed charges, approximately 50% of those total accounts will be sitting on your books at one time, rolling over throughout the months.

So, 50% of the total annual collection of billed charges for our sample practice would be $74,000 sitting on the books each month. If you lose 10% of the worth of that money, that represents a loss of $7,400: 10% of $74,000 = $7,400.

If you could have had that money in hand, you could have either invested it or serviced debts. Then your money would have been working for you rather than decreasing in value.

Let's add all of that up. Remember, this practice had a $7,400 loss of the dollar, plus $29,600 uncollectibles, for a total of $37,000. Add in the direct cost of billing and collecting of $17,610. This total is $54,610. That is how much it costs a $740,000 practice to run a credit business over a year's time. What percentage is $54,610 of the $148,000 credit business? 37%!

### Receivables Management Cost

| | |
|---|---|
| Accounts Receivable 10% of 74,000 | $7400 |
| Uncollected Revenue 20% of $120,000 | $29,600 |
| Cost for Billed Charges TOTAL: | $17,610 $54,610 |
| 37 % of Billed Charges | |

© Dr. T. Warren Center

## RECEIVABLE MANAGEMENT COSTS

Let that soak in just a minute—37%. The average general dental practice has an overhead between 65% to 70% (or more, according to some surveys). If it costs 37% to manage the credit aspect of the practice, and the overhead of the practice is 65-70%, guess what? You're breaking even or losing money on the credit business portion of your practice. That makes no sense.

**KEY POINT: Get out of the banking business. Put the banking aspect or the credit aspect of your business into the hands of professionals, professional people who spend every day working with patients and their accounts**. These specialists who manage the healthcare financing programs have the professional ability to collect gently but firmly with the persistence that must be applied to obtain effective collection.

Again, referring to the ADA, **approximately 30.8% of the people in the United States have not visited the dentist or gone to a dental clinic in the past year.**

According to the American Dental Association's Survey Center's Public Opinion Surveys, here are the main reasons people had for not going to the dentist more often.

1.  **"IT COSTS TOO MUCH!"** There is the number one reason for people not seeking dental care. Could we also say that this is the number one reason for not accepting the treatment once it has been presented? Probably!

    Offering a healthcare/patient financing program will help both you and your patients deal with the **"costs too much"** barrier. Patients will be able to accept treatment that otherwise might have been rejected or delayed. You will be able to increase production significantly because of your ability to overcome the barrier of cost. Both parties win.

2.  Also, if you are able to accomplish more dentistry per appointment and see the patient for fewer visits, that helps both parties deal with the second real issue: **"TIME."** The survey shows that time is a concern to people: convenient hours, not having to wait, having more important things to do. Being able to schedule longer appointments and doing more dentistry per appointment when and where appropriate reduces the amount of time and the number of visits a person needs to make. Remember that MODEL OF SUCCESS!

    And, certainly, practicing this way is a very profitable way to practice dentistry. And, that's what you want—to practice in not only a productive manner—but also a profitable manner.

## A NEW TEAM MEMBER

Think of your patient financing company and the professionals who manage these accounts as your "financial partner." You are going to pay a salary, in essence, to a professional organization and to qualified people to manage the credit portion of your practice. Spend your time doing what you do best: dentistry. Let the pros handle the money management for your patients.

The available healthcare financing programs are different in protocol, but the vast majority of them are going to have a service charge. That service charge ranges from about 4% to 15% (depending on the type of program a patient selects). Many practitioners think "Oh, no, that's terrible. That's too much. I'm not going to pay that much."

However, look at this in a new light. By carrying accounts on your own books, it is costing you approximately 37%. If a company will handle or manage the credit aspect of your practice for anywhere from 4 to 15%, you are saving an incredible amount of money in overhead. Instead of 37%, it is going to cost you 4% to 15%.

If a person indicates that he/she needs to make small payments and spread those payments out over a period of time, you would introduce your financing program.

> **Team Member:** *Ms. Jones, I understand that you feel concerned about the investment you will be making. Many of our patients have felt the same concern until they found out that we do offer long-term financing in our practice. We work with ABC Financing Company. You complete an application right here in our practice—you don't have to go anywhere. Once you have completed the application, we can provide the necessary information to the company to see about establishing a line of credit for you. Once that line of credit is established, we can begin your treatment. You will then be able to make small monthly payments and spread the payments over a long period of time. You will only be required to make a minimum payment each month.*

Once the patient is extended a line of credit, finance their dentistry. Complete a charge slip and submit for payment. You will receive payment for the services minus the service fee where this applies. Most of the time, the funds are electronically placed into your bank account. Direct deposit (EFT) is usually available. In fact, now with certain companies and with certain software programs, you can process payments right online in your practice. This just gets more and more convenient.

The patient begins making payments to the financing program. They no longer owe the dentist. If the patient defaults on the account for any reason at all, the dentist is in no way responsible for the account ever again. The programs are non-recourse and place the dentist at no risk whatsoever.

Remember the scenario of the $740,000 practice? Historically, dental practices have been writing off approximately 20% of the credit portion of their revenues. But, if you allow a professional financing company to handle that portion of your practice, you will not experience that kind of loss.

> **Example:** Take a $1000 charge, and let's say the service fee to you is 5%. You would receive a check for $950. That

would be the end of that. You would not send statements. You would not handle collection issues. You would receive your money. Think of this service fee as the salary you are paying the company to work for you in essence. They are the financial vehicle for your patient to pay for their dental care, if need be. These are excellent programs and deserve your careful study and attention.

While working with over 2,500 dental practices, we at Jameson Management, Inc., have seen significant increases in productivity (10-40%) when a practice uses a financing program well. We help practices not only get involved with patient financing, but also learn how to use the programs effectively.

If I asked you how much dentistry you had sitting in your charts waiting to be done, what would you say? Many dentists say that they have more dentistry sitting in their charts than they have ever provided. Offering this type of program will get some of that dentistry out of the charts and into the mouths of your patients.

## CHAPTER FIVE

# MAXIMIZING A HEALTHCARE FINANCING PROGRAM: MARKETING

*"There is only one boss: the customer. And he can fire everyone in the company from the chairman on down, simply by spending his money somewhere else."*

**—Sam Walton, Founder, Wal-Mart Stores, Inc.**

So, you've become involved with a healthcare/patient financing program, but you're not quite sure what to do with it. You expected to see some practice growth and some financial reward from the program, but that isn't happening yet. You're wondering what you can do to achieve both of these goals: practice growth and financial reward. In this chapter, I'll explain seven ways to develop your practice using patient financing. In addition, I will suggest some verbal skills for explaining the program and for defusing some of the objections your patients will express. Follow these recommendations as outlined, and you can increase revenues in your practice anywhere from 10% to 40%.

How much are you producing now? Would a 10% increase make a difference for you? And what would happen with a 40% increase? The data behind this kind of statement is valid. For most practices, there is a great deal of dentistry sitting in the charts waiting to be done. That doesn't mean you have done anything wrong. It means that something has prevented people from moving ahead. A person wouldn't come to your practice if they didn't want or need something. So, if they walk out the door not scheduling an appointment—something went wrong. There are four major reasons people do not proceed with treatment:

1. No trust

2. No need

3. No urgency

4. No value

In order for people to say "yes" to treatment and to separate themselves from their hard earned money, one, or a combination of these four major factors must be emphatically in place. And, certainly, you can flip these around and if a patient did not proceed with treatment, one of these four principles, or a combination of them was missing.

If a person perceives the value of the treatment, sees the need, understands the urgency, and trusts the doctor and team, they will go ahead if they can afford it. That's where your financial system comes into place to support the process.

Determine the value of your average treatment plan. If one more person per week proceeds with treatment because they can afford it, what would that mean to you? Take that average treatment plan fee, and multiply that by 4 weeks in the month. Now multiply that by 12 months in the year and see what that would mean to the productivity of the practice.

**For Example:** If one person per week goes ahead with $500 worth of treatment, let's see what that looks like for you.

$500 per week
x 4 weeks in the month
___
$2,000 per month
x 12
___
$24,000 per year

**Or,**

What if *one person a day* proceeded with $500 worth of treatment because they had a convenient way to pay?

$500 per day
x200 days per year (average in the country)
___
**$100,000 per year of additional revenue**

This *could* occur if only one person per day goes ahead with a minimal amount of treatment because they can spread out the payments and not have to come up with a large amount at one time. (And I am talking about $500—not $5,000.)

This is an extremely profitable treatment to provide. You won't be increasing your overhead by much, and you will be doing more dentistry, which is what you want. About 20% of the increased production will be additional costs. However, about 80% drops to the bottom line.

## PROMOTING PATIENT FINANCING: IDEAS TO CONSIDER

Remember the staggering information about credit cards and the reason why people don't use credit cards in a dental office? Because they didn't know their doctor accepted credit cards. Well, the same thing is true about patient financing. Your patients don't know!

Give the following marketing and promotion ideas a try. They work! Think this through. Multiply your present productivity by 10-40% increase without increasing overhead significantly. Increased profit margin.

If you do the following things the way I describe them, you can have that kind of increase. Make sure that when you are placing any marketing strategies into action that you track the results. When a new patient comes to your practice, find out how they found out about you and record that in your software. Then, review this to see which of your marketing strategies is working the best. If something you are doing is not getting the results you desire, make alterations. If something is getting fantastic results, make sure you continue!

## 1. INTRODUCE THE PROGRAM TO YOUR ENTIRE PATIENT FAMILY

In a special mailing, or in your newsletter, tell your existing patient family about the financing program. Present the program in an exciting, informative manner, one that stresses the benefits to the patient. (SUPPLEMENTAL MANUAL: 5.1)

**(Figure 5.1: Newsletter of Dr. Jill Wade and Dr. Kristy Moody, Stonebriar Smile Design, Frisco, Texas)**

In this special mailing, include a brochure about the financing program; some offices include an application. Make it easy for the patient to become involved. Eliminate as many barriers as possible.

Some patients in your practice will not need the program. If they don't need financial assistance, they won't apply. However, "Fear of Cost" is the number one reason people don't come to the dentist, so there you have it! Some patients may have completed one phase of treatment but don't schedule the next phase because they owe you money or they can't handle a major outlay of cash. In either case establishing a line of credit may dissolve that barrier of cost. With a line of credit from your financing program, they may be willing and able to go ahead.

---

**KEY POINT: Get the information about your financing program into the hands of your consumers—the patients.**

---

Practices spend a great deal of time and money trying to get new patients. Of course, this is critical. However, nurture your existing patients. Are patients falling through the cracks as fast as they are coming in as new patients? Do you know? If this is happening, your practice will either plateau or spiral downward. Maximize your market share by focusing on having patients say yes to treatment, both new patients and patients of record.

## NEWSLETTERS

Newsletters? Are they effective? Yes! One of your main commissions as a dental professional is to educate. One of the best ways to educate your patient family, next to your in-office one-on-one education, is through a patient newsletter.

Good marketing recommends that you stay in contact with your customer base, your patient family, on a regular basis. At each contact introduce them to something new and reinforce something that is important to your business. **Repetition is a key to learning** so continuing to address opportunities, including payment opportunities, is essential.

---

### KEY POINT: REPETITION IS THE KEY TO LEARNING AND THE KEY TO YOUR SUCCESS WITH YOUR PATIENT FINANCING PROGRAM.

---

With your newsletter, you will do the following:

1. Be in the homes of your patient families in a positive way on a regular basis.

2. Inform your patients about what's happening in dentistry. Don't "assume" that patients know about new and improved types of treatment. They don't. It is your responsibility and opportunity to educate your patients and community about the new advances in dentistry.

3. Let your patient family know what you are doing in your practice to keep abreast of the latest and best in healthcare for their benefit.

4. Inform them of the convenient financing options available today.

5. Express your appreciation for their confidence in you.

6. Invite them to refer their family, colleagues, and friends to you.

Your newsletter needs to be economical and efficient both in time and money. The digital/patient communication systems that intertwine with your computer software make this so easy. You will want to individualize the look and content of your newsletter. Some of the content provided by the companies is just fine, but research shows that when you personalize the content results are better. Your logo and branding will be uniquely yours. Assign a person in your practice to be the "marketing champion" so that they will make sure the newsletter is created and digitally sent to your patient family in a timely fashion. Make it good, pretty, and interesting so that people will want to read it.

**(Figure 5.2)**

Some practices send their newsletters both digitally and in hard copy. The benefit of the hard copy, although this does add cost, is that the newsletter will be sitting in the house for others to see. Potential referrals! Or, your patients can hand it to other people for the same purpose, nurturing referrals. Ideally, you will have approximately 70% of your new patients coming to you as personal referrals and about 30% coming from external marketing strategies.

**When we became involved with patient financing, we produced one entire issue on the subject to introduce the program. Then, in every issue, we reintroduce the fact that we provide financing, just to keep that fresh in patients' minds.**

In October of every year, we recommend sending a letter to patients reminding them that if they have not utilized or taken advantage of the yearly maximum of their insurance, now is a good time to do so.

If they have existing dentistry that needs to be completed, we encourage them to maximize their insurance benefits. Rather than wait until the end of the year, a very hectic time for us, we encourage them to call now to schedule an appointment for that dentistry. Again, to maximize their insurance, we also tell them that if they have any concerns about the balance after insurance pays, we have comfortable and convenient financing available for them. (SUPPLEMENTAL MANUAL: 5.2)

In January of every year, we remind our patients that a new year has begun and that this new year indicates a new maximum for their insurance. Therefore, if they have incomplete treatment, or if they or members of their family need continuous care, this new year offers the new insurance benefits. We encourage them to use this wonderful supplement to their dental care and that they can finance the balance after the insurance pays. Or if they don't have dental insurance, we have a comfortable, convenient way to finance their dentistry.

## PROFESSIONALLY PRODUCED NEWSLETTERS

There are numerous companies that produce patient education news-letters for practices. These are beautifully and professionally prepared and fulfill all the criteria I outlined above. In these professionally produced newsletters, space is reserved for your own name and practice, logo, and an article or relevant data pertaining to your practice. This individualizes the newsletter for you.

(Figure 5.3)

Any of these methods are great. The point here is that constant contact with clients is beneficial and needs to be maintained. You select the method that best suits you. These, too, can be digitized.

My definition of good marketing is educating patients about what is happening in dentistry-and what you are doing to stay on top of the very best. Newsletters are a great place to invest a small portion of your marketing budget.

Your new patient flow will increase as patients become involved with a financing program. People will go home and say, "Hey, my dentist has this new program available. You can finance your dentistry and pay it out. The payments are real small." Personal referrals will always be your best source for new patients. We have found that many patients are coming to us because they now know about the comfortable, convenient financing we offer. Good dentistry. Good doctor. Good Team. Good financing. A great combination.

In addition, to the initial introduction of the program through a special mailing or a patient education newsletter, consider an introduction through a practice brochure.

**(Figure 5.4: Brochure of Dr. Mark Hyman of Greensboro, NC)**

You can also introduce your financial options on your patient information sheet. We send this information sheet/health history to patients prior to their arrival for their first appointment. Include information about your financing program in your Welcome Packet. (SUPPLEMENTAL MANUAL: 5.3)

This Welcome Packet can be sent in hard copy through the mail or created and sent digitally. Some marketing experts recommend that you send it both ways. Be sure to ask your patients how they would like to receive it. Remember—one third of Americans don't have the Internet. The Welcome Packet includes the practice brochure, the information sheet/health history form, along with a self-addressed envelope, a card confirming the appointment, a patient education newsletter, a Smile Evaluation Form, and information about our financing program. We send this to a patient as soon as he/she calls to schedule a new patient evaluation. (SUPPLEMENTAL MANUAL: 5.4)

We introduce the Welcome Packet to patients in the following manner:

> **Business Administrator:** *Ms. Jones, I'm going to be sending you some information about our practice before you arrive. I am sending you a card confirming your appointment and a brochure about our practice. We want you to know about us before you get here. Also, I am including your patient information sheet, health history form along with a self-addressed stamped envelope, AND A SMILE EVALUATION FORM. Please complete this form and send it back to us before your appointment. We have found that our patients are more comfortable filling this out at home where they have all the necessary data and plenty of time. In addition, if you send it back to us prior to your appointment, the doctor will be able to review the information and be better prepared for your appointment. Plus, I will be able to enter all the information into the computer and we will be able to seat you more quickly. I know your time is valuable.*

New patients see immediately that convenient financing is available since this is addressed in the brochure and on HH/Information sheet. It is presented in a very positive way. There is no question or confusion. Everything is spelled out before the fact. Up front is the best way to deal with any arrangement. Dr. Burt Press, former president of the ADA, has told us for a long time to "inform before you perform." That applies to the treatment to be rendered and to the financial responsibility. Inform patients of your financial options right from the start. People are glad to know! Defuse possible "fear of cost" before the fact.

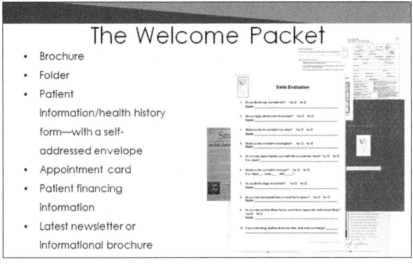

# The Welcome Packet

- Brochure
- Folder
- Patient information/health history form—with a self-addressed envelope
- Appointment card
- Patient financing information
- Latest newsletter or informational brochure

**(Figure 5.5)**

## Yellow Pages

If you utilize the Yellow Page ads, it is a good idea to let people know you have comfortable financing available. Yellow Pages can be printed or digital or both. While Yellow Pages are not as popular nor as vital as they were historically, however, they are still used as a resource, and if you are going to participate, you need to do this well. Here are some key points regarding yellow pages ads:

1.   Use a professional design team or your own professional marketing consultants. Do not use the Yellow Pages personnel for the design of your ad.

2.   Make sure you are using a directory that is just right for you, your market, and your area. Don't choose a directory just because it might be the least expensive, choose a directory because it will get you the best results.

3.   In the ad itself use color to attract attention. Use the color, logo, type of print, etc., that is your "brand." You want the same image to be evident in all of your marketing, both internally and externally.

4. Have a headline that grabs the attention of the reader, the person seeking a dentist in your area.

5. Use a great photo or illustration that is relevant, pleasant, and eye-catching.

6. Focus your content on the benefits of coming to your practice. Remember that all behavior is driven by "what's in this for me!" Don't go on and on about the procedures you offer, that's not what's going to draw a patient to you. Talk about how pleasant the experience will be: your friendly team, your beautiful environment, convenience, and **MAKE SURE YOU FOCUS ON AFFORDABLE/COMFORTABLE FINANCING!**

7. Decide what your target market is and design your ad accordingly. For example, if you want to do comprehensive restorative and aesthetics, don't have a photo of children in your ad!

8. Make your ad easy to read, no fancy fonts. Make it simple and well-organized, and let the potential patient FIND YOU EASILY, BOTH WITH AN ACCESSIBLE PHONE NUMBER AND ADDRESS OR DIRECTIONS.

## 2. ACCOUNTS RECEIVABLE TRANSFER

If you have existing accounts receivable, consider making an active effort to transfer as many of those accounts as possible to cash, to a bankcard or to a financing program, if this is a good account where people have been making payments. Do not use your patient financing program as a collection agency for delinquent accounts. There are other companies that do that.

Cut your costs of operation by letting professionals take over the management of accounts receivable. When people owe you money, they may delay further treatment or continuous care. However, if they have a line of credit for dentistry, they will, as research has proven, move ahead with treatment or stay more regular with continuous care.

### SUGGESTED STEPS FOR THIS TRANSFER:

1. Analyze your accounts receivable. Determine the following:

   a. How much is insurance? How much is private pay?

b. Of the private pay accounts, how much is 30, 60, 90 (or more) days past due?

c. Those accounts that are extremely past due and have had no activity whatsoever, may need to be turned over for legal action. Make sure the dentist approves all accounts to be turned over or written off. Be certain that you have made a concerted effort to collect the account and that the patient has been unwilling to negotiate a settlement of the account before you turn anything over for collection.

2. For the remaining accounts, create a letter introducing the idea of transferring accounts to the Healthcare Financing Program. (SUPPLEMENTAL MANUAL: 5.5) Expound on the benefits of the program, such as:

a. Longer time in which to pay the account.

b. Smaller monthly payments.

c. No large payments due at one time.

d. No initial or yearly fee to become involved with the program.

e. Available credit for emergencies or for necessary and desired treatment.

3. Send an application and a brochure with this letter. Send this letter in a separate mailing rather than with statements. Place the letter on your professional stationery and place it in one of your personalized envelopes. This needs to be a special mailing so that it receives special attention from your patients.

You may wish to offer a 10% courtesy if the guarantor comes in and pays his/her balance in full within 30 days of the postmark of the letter. This, in itself, may bring in a great number of payments. (The cost of carrying the account on your own books will be greater than the courtesy given.)

4. Once you have sent your first mailing, begin a telephone campaign to all of those patients who do not respond.

> **Business Administrator**: *Good Morning, Ms. Jones. This is Cathy from Dr. Jameson's dental office. I'm so glad I have been able to reach you this morning. Ms. Jones, last month we mailed*

*some information to you about a new healthcare financing program that we have available in our office. Did you receive that information?*

*You did. Great. Ms. Jones, our records indicate that you have a balance with our practice of $_____. We've found that our patients are more comfortable with smaller monthly payments that they can spread out over a longer period of time. That is exactly what this new program lets our patients do.*

*When you apply and are extended a line of credit, you can transfer your existing balance to our new financing program (NAME OF COMPANY). Then, we can transfer your existing balance and your first monthly payment will be approximately $_____.*

*Does this sound like a program that would be of interest to you?*

*Great. Can you come by the office and complete the application on our computer? Or, if you choose, I can give you the information and you can go directly to our website and apply for a line of credit with our patient financing company. You will see the portal for that company right on our website. We will be informed as soon as your line of credit is established, and we can work together to transfer your balance.*

*This line of credit will be yours and will also let you proceed with your necessary hygienic care and any other treatment that you and Dr. Jameson feel is appropriate.*

*We appreciate you so much, Ms. Jones, and always enjoy working with you. We think this is one of the best services we have been able to offer to our patients. Now, let's decide how you would like to proceed.*

(Also in the SUPPLEMENTAL MANUAL: 5.6)

Track your telephone calls. Make notes of who you have called, those who were sent an application, the date you sent the application, the date it was received back in the office, and any comments relative to the conversation. (SUPPLEMENTAL MANUAL: 5.7)

Please note: The sooner you can contact someone in person or by phone the better. Any time you are in contact with the patient is a good time to encourage them to work with you to transfer their balance. Be faithful with your encouragement of this transfer. The best way to collect is face to face. The second best way is over the phone. The third best way is through the written word.

5. At the next statement run (another month has passed) send a follow-up letter, with another brochure and another application to anyone who has not yet transferred their account. (SUPPLEMENTAL MANUAL: 5.8) In this letter, let your patients know you have changed accounting methods and are offering this financial service to those who wish to extend their payments over a long period of time. Once again, stress the benefits of the program and the benefits to the individuals.

   Continue your telephone campaign.

6. By now, you should have a strong response to your efforts, especially if you followed the above recommended regime carefully and with commitment. If you are not going to follow the campaign through to the end with consistency, don't expect a great response. In fact, if you aren't prepared to take this campaign through all the above recommended steps, you shouldn't even begin it. You can only access good results if you do this correctly.

7. Continue your telephone campaign until you have contacted every person who has an accounts receivable with you.

**KEY POINT: Many offices have converted half of their accounts receivable to cash in a three-to six-month period of time. Results are in direct correlation to effort put forth.**

**NOTE:** If a patient is abiding by a previously agreed upon financial arrangement, go ahead and offer the program to him/her, but willingly allow him/her to maintain their agreement if it is comfortable.

If you are accepting assignments of benefits of insurance, maintain an accounts receivable of no more than half of your average monthly production. If you follow the financial protocol outlined in this book, and if you are managing the insurance system excellently (again, see

Dr. Charles Blair's books on managing insurance and on coding), you should have no accounts receivable other than insurance. Remember, the ADA data shows that the average practice in America has about half of its monthly income coming in the form of an insurance check, that's the half I am referring to that would be acceptable accounts receivable. If you are using the other options, there would be no accounts receivable. Using EFT would be the exception.

With careful management, you should have an approximate seven to ten working-day turnaround on all your insurance claims and should have no claims 30 days or more past due.

Practices that are not accepting assignment of benefits from insurance companies should have no accounts receivable. In fact, these practices may have healthy credit because many patients are paying in advance in order to receive the accounting reduction/cash courtesy.

The team will love the accounts receivable transfer because they are going to get out of the statement and collection business. This gives them more time to take care of other necessary duties which are much more productive for the practice. Patients will accept the accounts receivable transfer because most patients would rather owe a financing institution than owe the dentist. In addition, their payments will probably be less per month.

Will abiding by this financial protocol hurt productivity? **No!** The practices we work with increase production by an average of over 40% within a year to 18 months from the time we begin consulting with them. And, they certainly become more profitable. When this financial system is implemented, stress is relieved because the money from production is in the bank and is not sitting out there doing nothing. More time is available for the important activities that build the practice, time is not spent on statements and collection.

Some dentists are concerned that patients will be upset if the financial protocol is firm, yet flexible. My experience has been this: once you set a financial protocol and your patients understand that this will serve them better, to offer top quality dentistry with comfortable financial options, they will be fine. Let them know you had to get out of the banking business because it was not financially feasible for you to run a banking business within your practice. Maintain your commitment to quality. They will respect this.

# 3. CHART AUDITING

Most dentists will agree that there is a great deal of dentistry sitting in the charts waiting to be done. "Fear of cost" is probably the major barrier. Certainly, no perceived need is also a major barrier. But, as my dear friend Jeff Gelona, an outstanding coach and trainer, used to say, "When a person says 'no' to your offer, ask them, 'Is that no for now or no forever?'"

Review your files/treatment plans to see who has dentistry that has been diagnosed but is incomplete. You may be able to either reactivate people into the practice or enable people to go ahead with the next phase of treatment especially when you introduce the healthcare financing program.

I am going to describe a way to fully audit your charts and then I am going to recommend a way to audit your charts on a daily basis.

## Suggested Procedure for a Full Audit of the Charts

1.  Set a goal and follow the process of goal accomplishment as taught in Chapter Two.

    **Example**

    a.  The team sets the goal. They determine the end result they expect and intend to accomplish with the chart audit.

    b.  The objectives and strategies of how the team is going to accomplish the goal are defined. What are they going to do? How are they going to do it?

    c.  The person or persons responsible for each specific task are assigned their detailed duties.

    d.  The time frame is set. Time activate each step.

    e.  Evaluate. You must be able to evaluate your progress and your success. Therefore, the monitor becomes critical. Otherwise, how can you measure your progress?

        Let's say that the clinical assistant is going to be doing the actual auditing of the charts, and the business administrator is going to make the telephone calls. Now, follow along with my example. (SUPPLEMENTAL MANUAL: 5.9) They are going to make every effort to audit 20 charts per week. They feel that this is a comfortable number for them. They are going to evaluate their progress and give a report at their weekly team meeting to show the entire team the results of these audits. They will be evaluating: (1) how many patients were contacted (2) how many of these patients scheduled an appointment either with the dentist or with the hygienist and (3) if patients were unwilling to schedule, what were the predominant reasons. Having this vital information shows where improvement or extra attention needs to be directed.

Gather the following information on each patient:

- The date the person was called
- The person's name
- Telephone number
- The last date seen
- Details of any dentistry diagnosed but left incomplete
- If the patient has insurance or not
- Details about their policy
- If the patient is a part of the healthcare financing program at this time or not, and/or how much their first monthly payment would be if they financed
- If the person is interested in the financing program, the date the application was sent is noted
- The next column is the date the application is returned
- And the last column is for comments

  (SUPPLEMENTAL MANUAL: 5.10 and 5.11, Tracking Devices for Chart Auditing)

2. Once the data has been gathered for "this week's charts," make courteous marketing telephone calls to those patients to: (1) express your concern about their care, (2) let them know you have not forgotten them, (3) reinforce the need for treatment, and (4) explain your new financing program.

**Don't audit any more charts until these patients have been called. Some people audit all the charts but don't make any phone calls. What's the purpose?**

Approach this effort steadily and with a positive attitude. Business tells us that 64% of people promoting a service or a product never ask a potential customer/client to proceed. You never know what you will get until you ask! The law of averages will work in your favor if you work on your entire set of charts.

Don't become discouraged if everyone doesn't jump at the idea. They won't. If you get a positive response from 20-30 percent of the people contacted, you will have served your purpose well. Everyone will be a winner—you, the practice, and, most of all, the patient. At this time, you can introduce your healthcare financing program, so that you can clear the way for that patient to come in and say "yes" to the dentistry.

For example, you audit a chart and find that a person has some necessary dentistry that has been diagnosed but remains incomplete.

> **BA:** *Ms. Jones? This is Cathy, from Dr. Jameson's dental office. I'm glad I have been able to reach you. Ms. Jones, Dr. Jameson has been reviewing your records and realized that the treatment he has recommended for you has not been completed and he was concerned. You are missing a tooth on the lower left area of your mouth and the adjacent teeth are shifting, and both you and the doctor are concerned about the potential loss of more teeth. He asked that I call you to see if you had any questions about the treatment that he has prescribed.*
>
> *I'm also calling to tell you about an exciting new program that we have available in our practice. Ms. Jones, we have become involved with a program that allows our patients to "finance" their dentistry and pay it out over a period of time with very small monthly payments. I see that you have dental insurance through XYZ Company and that is great. Dental insurance has been so helpful and serves as a great supplement to your dental care. Our new program lets you finance your dental care, including the balance that insurance does not cover.*
>
> *In reviewing your record, I see that the fee for the treatment Dr. Jameson is recommending for you is approximately $2,300. We estimate your insurance company will pay about*

*$1,000. Therefore, we could file your insurance as a service to you, and for about $35 per month you could finance the remaining balance. You could spread the payments out over a period of time, keep the payments small and comfortable, not put yourself under any financial stress, and best of all you could proceed with the treatment that both you and the doctor believe is best for you. Would this be something of interest to you?*

Then she will say "yes" or "no" or she might have some other questions to ask you about the program or about the dentistry.

She might say, "Yes, this sounds good to me. I have wanted to have this done, but there was no way I could afford it. I don't have $1,300. But I can pay $35 a month".

**BA's response:** *Ms. Jones, you can go right to our website and locate the portal for our patient financing company. It's called XYZ Company. You can complete your application right there on our website. It's quite easy to complete. Once they have established a line of credit for you, we can schedule an appointment to begin your treatment. How does that sound?*

If a patient wants you to send them an application through the mail, that is fine, or you can do this digitally. However, any time an application goes out of your office, through traditional mail or email, track the date that the application is sent and follow up!

Again, look at the tracking sheet. Note the date you sent the application. If you notice that you sent Ms. Jones an application but that you have not received the application back in the office, that is an alert. It is time to make a phone call to Ms. Jones.

**BA:** *Ms. Jones? This is Cathy from Dr. Jameson's office. I sent an application to your home regarding our healthcare financing plan and I haven't received that application back in the office. I wondered if you had received it. Oh, you have? Good. Do you have any questions or is there anything I can do to help?*

*No? Then just drop that back in the mail and we will get it processed. I look forward to receiving the application. When I do receive the information, I will make sure that it is taken care of quickly. Once we find that you have been extended a credit line, I'll contact you and we will schedule an appointment to begin your treatment.*

The tracking monitor will let you know when an application has left the office and when it is returned. Otherwise, you can see how a lot of information could fall through the cracks. Evaluation, or monitoring, is like taking the temperature of the practice. If you see that the temperature is rising or if the monitors are indicating negative information, this is a symptom of a disease. This measurement gives you a chance to do something about it. If you don't track information about your practice, you lose the opportunity to correct any problems.

Also, track this chart audit and the mailing of your applications. Otherwise the applications will be floating around and you won't have any idea where they are. All of this applies to your digital tracking as well.

When you do reach a person, whether or not they wish to become involved with your financing program, you will want to either schedule the patients for treatment with the dentist or with the hygienist for continuous care. Most dentists feel that if the diagnosis has been made in the last six months, it is appropriate to schedule treatment with the dentist. However, if the patient has not been seen in the last six months, he/she needs to be scheduled for a periodic evaluation with the dentist as well as a professional dental cleaning with the hygienist. A new diagnosis and treatment plan would be necessary.

Don't try to audit all of the charts at once. Audit on a regular basis, consistently, and with a plan. Then, get on the phone and make contact with those patients. You are going to take many small steps and pretty soon you will have completed the long walk. What a fantastic way to expand your practice and to maximize your new financing program.

## DAILY CHART AUDITS THROUGH A HEALTHY MORNING MEETING

There are many important parts to a productive morning meeting, but one of those parts is to identify dentistry that has been diagnosed but not completed. Most practices will find that between 50-75% of patients coming to the office on any given day need some treatment beyond today, either with the hygienist or the dentist. Instead of spending a great deal of time during the morning meeting talking about what you will be doing that day, make note of what the patient needs next. Then when the patient is in the treatment area, have a conversation with him or her about the next phase of necessary dentistry. Use the intra-oral or digital camera to show the patient the next area of concern. Stress the benefits of proceeding with treatment and discuss any problems that may arise if the person doesn't proceed.

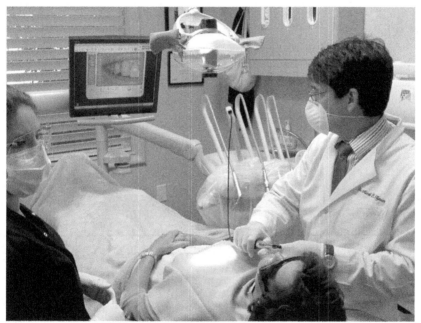

(Figure 5.6)

Your goal is to have more people saying "yes" to treatment that has been diagnosed but has not yet been provided. Get the dentistry out of the charts and into the mouths of your patients. Remember, your doctor would not diagnose and recommend treatment if the patient didn't need it. You do the patient a great service by continuing to encourage them to proceed. This may be a good time to introduce your patient financing program. You will be able to do this face-to face.

In essence, by doing this on a daily basis at your morning meeting, the entire team is sharing in the responsibility of doing ongoing chart audits.

KEY POINT: Most practices can schedule more dentistry from any given day than they are providing in that day. In addition to identifying necessary care, become great educators of dentistry to help people understand the benefits of oral health and beautiful smiles.

# 4. INSURANCE

As you do your chart audit, you may find that many people are putting off their dental treatment even if they have dental insurance. Available benefits are not being used. These people may not be able to handle the estimated patient portion, or co-pay. If you are taking assignment of benefits, when you contact these people during your chart audit, let them know you will file their insurance as a service to them. Tell them that if they would like to spread out the balance after insurance pays, that you have a new, convenient way for them to do just that. Then, tell them about your financing program.

On an ongoing basis, tell your insured patients about this opportunity to utilize insurance benefits and have convenient monthly payments for the estimated patient portion. **More of your patients will use their insurance benefits.**

If you are not taking insurance on assignment, but rather patients are paying you in full and being reimbursed by the insurance company directly, terrific. However, some people may choose to finance their entire treatment so that the monthly payments will be comfortable for them. That's fine. Both of you win.

> **Business Administrator:** *Ms. Jones, it sounds to me like you do want to receive the treatment that the doctor is recommending to you but that you need to spread the payments out over a period of time to keep the monthly payments comfortable for you and your family. That's very understandable. For that reason, we work with a patient financing program. Once you receive payment from your insurance company, you can make a substantial payment to the finance company, which will lower your balance and your monthly payment. Let's fill out the application now. It will just take a couple of minutes and I will be more than happy to help you.*

# 5. CONTINUOUS CARE/HYGIENE

At Jameson Management, we consider the hygiene department the "lifeblood of the practice." This is where you get people healthy and keep them healthy. This is where you can also do the following:

1. reinforce the value of dentistry diagnosed but incomplete

2. identify new areas of concern since the last appointment

3. identify periodontal concerns and once the doctor has diagnosed, make recommendations for appropriate treatment

4. introduce options for advanced restorative treatment

5. introduce aesthetic alternatives

Using an intra-oral camera is imperative since 83% of learning takes place visually. People will benefit and be more likely to move ahead if they can see what is going on in their own mouth and can see before and after photos of what you are doing in your own practice.

Many people don't stay on a regular program of continuous care in hygiene, or they do not involve all members of their family in your program because the investment is prohibitive. That's the last thing you want—for your patients to put off needed or desired care because of the cost.

Introducing the financing program to your hygiene patients or through your hygiene retention program will not only allow more of your patients to receive this valuable service, but it will also help you nurture this lifeblood of your practice—the hygiene department.

If you are involved with a non-surgical periodontal program, or if you are offering sealant therapy, you know that many patients want and need this care but find the financial responsibility difficult. However, if they find they can receive this care and the monthly investment will fit nicely into the family budget, many will proceed. A letter addressing this opportunity is included in the Supplemental Manual. (SUPPLEMENTAL MANUAL: 5.13)

Make an effort to have 85-90% of your active patient family regularly engaged in hygiene. (The ADA defines an active patient as someone who has been in the practice to receive care in the past 2 years). Find out accurately what your retention ratio is at the present time, and set a goal to increase that by 5-10% or more! Data shows that approximately 40-60% of a doctor's restorative or aesthetic dentistry is provided on hygiene patients who proceed with previously diagnosed treatment or who move ahead with something new. Patient financing will help you with this.

# 6. CASE PRESENTATION

The human mind can only think of one thing at a time. Therefore, if a patient is calculating what they think the treatment will cost, they may not hear a word you are saying during a consultation. Don't hesitate to introduce your financing program during, or before, your clinical recommendations. Otherwise, as you are trying to educate the patient about the services you are offering, they may be thinking of nothing but the cost.

---

**KEY POINT: Addressing a potential negative before the fact, gives you a chance to turn that potential negative into a positive.**

---

**Example**

**Doctor:** *Ms. Jones, before I tell you what I have diagnosed and before I explain the treatment I believe would be best for you, let me tell you that if you have any concern about the financing of the dentistry, we have convenient financial options right here in our practice. Before we proceed with treatment, we will make sure that you are comfortable with the financing of the treatment. But for right now, I would like to discuss the treatment I feel would be best for you. Let's focus on those recommendations and then we will discuss the financing thoroughly. Does that sound good to you?*

Or, if a person walks into a consultation room and before you even open your mouth to start making recommendations, they look at you and say something like, "Hey Doc, just get to the bottom line. Just tell me how much this is going to cost me." Answer their question with a question to clarify what they are asking.

**Doctor:** *Are you concerned about the financing of your dental care?*

**Patient**: *Sure. I'm sure this is going to cost an arm and a leg.*

---

**Dr.:** *Are you concerned about the total investment or finding a way to finance your care?*

**Patient**: *Well, a bit of both, I guess.*

**Doctor:** *I can appreciate that. That's why I have asked Jan, my treatment coordinator, to join us today. She will discuss the total investment and the options for payment we have available right here in our practice. I'm sure you and Jan will find an option that works well for you. But for now, if it's okay with you, I would like to focus on the clinical aspects of treatment—what I believe would be the best for you. Then, Jan will discuss the financial aspect of your care and our options. Is that okay?*

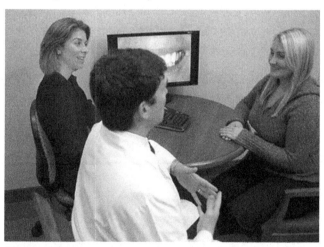

**(Figure 5.7)**

Once she has agreed, proceed with your clinical presentation. You have defused the fear of cost. The patient will be able to focus their attention on your clinical presentation. They will appreciate your empathy to their concern, and you will put the money questions where they belong.

**KEY POINT: Presenting the fee too early may be worse than not presenting the fee at all.**

The entire team has an essential role in the making of a financial arrangement. When a patient asks you a financial question in the clinical area, you must answer professionally and excellently. Without meaning to do so, you can undermine the business administrator's efforts to obtain a financial agreement by avoiding financial questions or by insinuating that discussions of money are taboo. If a patient asks anyone in the clinical area about finances, answer in the following manner:

*"Ms. Jones, it sounds like you are concerned about the financing of the treatment Dr. Jameson has recommended and I can appreciate that. Let me tell Jan, our Business Administrator, of your concern. We have outstanding financial options right here in our practice. I'm sure she will be able to find the one that works best for you. Once you and Jan arrange the financial aspect of care, would that make it possible for you to proceed with the treatment that Dr. Jameson has recommended, or do you have further questions for me?"*

Offer the best treatment possible, make the financing of the dentistry comfortable, and then get out of the way. Let the patient make the decision of whether or not to proceed.

**(Figure 5.8)**

## 7. SOCIAL MEDIA

*"Traditional marketing talks at people.*
*Content Marketing talks with them."*

**— Doug Kessler**

Carrie Webber is the Chief Communications Officer for The Jameson Group. She lectures throughout the United States and abroad on the subject of Marketing, including Social Media. In today's world of dentistry, or any business for that matter, social media has become the benchmark of relevant marketing. Social media allows a practice to communicate on a regular basis with patients in a cost-effective manner. In addition, while there is still time and expertise required for effective social media, just as there is with any marketing strategy, the time involved is less intensive.

CARRIE WEBBER, CHIEF COMMUNICATIONS OFFICER
JAMESON MANAGEMENT

Webber teaches what marketing experts have touted for years, which is the rule of seven. Patients may require five to seven "touches" or contacts with a practice or doctor before they actually pick up the phone and call to make an appointment, or go to the computer to schedule, if that is available. While personal referral remains the number one method of accessing new patients, other sources of generating new patients, or retaining existing patients, do include social media. A person may have heard about a practice through a personal referral. They may have received a brochure. They may have come across an online ad or a promotion in the community. But, the next step is often to go directly to the Internet and seek the website of the practice. Make sure yours is good—created and maintained by a professional marketing organization. Make sure that the organization has the capability to have your name and practice "pop up" on the first page of a search when a patient, or potential patient, seeks out information about you.

Your website needs to be easy to navigate, attractive, current, and patient-friendly. Make sure you are updating your information often and providing new material often enough that people, including your existing patients, will be interested in going back to your site often.

You will want to have a regular presence on social media outlets, including Facebook, Instagram, and YouTube. Make sure you are actively and consistently obtaining online reviews as an important element to your comprehensive efforts as well. Here again, the "marketing champion" in your practice will want to post regularly and to retrieve any responses to your posts so that questions or comments can be handled. Short, engaging videos of you, your team members, and patients (with written permission) grab the attention of people on social media. People/patients love to see what you are doing in the community, with charities, with schools, and in the practice. So while you can promote your dental services, remember that social media is just that—social. Educational? Yes. Social? Yes. Promotional? Yes. All of the above.

Certainly, as you are budgeting for marketing, you will want to include a specialist for your website. Please consider hiring a specialist in social media as well. In fact, a great marketing organization can and, in my opinion, should be a part of your team. You are dental professionals. Stick with that. Let a marketing pro become a vehicle for the promotion of your practice. If they are good, they will pay for themselves multi-fold.

Throughout your social media, you will want to promote the fact that you offer, accept, and encourage the use of patient financing. Once again, get the word out continuously.

# CHAPTER SIX

# EFFECTIVE FINANCIAL COMMUNICATION

*"Great communication makes it easier for doctors and teams to let patients know the benefits of patient financing and can encourage a patient to move forward with needed care."*
— DOUG HAMMOND, SENIOR VICE-PRESIDENT AND GENERAL MANAGER, Care Credit Core

Your financing program will work in direct proportion to your belief in the program as an asset to both practice and patients, and in your ability to communicate and market the program. (Refer to my book, *Great Communication = Great Production*, for further information on communication, including overcoming objections, refer to www.jamesonmanagement.com.)

Attitude is a choice. Choose to have a positive attitude about patient financing and your enthusiasm will come across to patients. You cannot buy enthusiasm, but you can catch it.

Communication skills can be learned. As a team, practice the communication skills I'm presenting in this chapter so that everyone is comfortable with them. Team members must be able to answer questions enthusiastically and competently. The more excited you are about your financing program, the more excited your patients will be. Result: the more receptive they will be to your suggestions. Patients will always reflect you.

Your success will be in direct proportion to your enthusiasm and to the success of your systems, including your financial systems.

## Making Successful Financial Agreements

Developing a financial agreement with a patient starts with the right mindset—a belief in both the care you are providing and in your financial services. Everyone on the team must believe that if a patient walks out the door not scheduling an appointment, the patient loses just as much as you do or more.

You want to develop a union between your practice and the patient, one in which both of you win. Arriving at an agreement about the equability of the fee as it relates to the dental care is what you want. Your job is to **find a solution** to the financial needs of the patients.

## 3 Essential Elements

Let's look at the following three essential elements:

1. **Knowledge of product and service.** Anyone developing a financial agreement must be comfortable answering clinical questions. This does not infer that you have to be a dentist to make a financial agreement, but you need to be aware of what the doctor is recommending, why he is recommending certain procedures, how long it will take and, of course, the financial responsibility. The person discussing the financial responsibility needs to be able to give the doctor third-party backup support. Patients may ask a team member questions they won't ask the doctor. Knowledge of the recommended treatment is valuable for the coordinator's confidence.

   When a patient asks things like, "Do you think I really need this?" Or, "Would you have this done if it were you?" Or, "Do you think this will hurt?" Or, "How long will this last?" Or, "Is there any other way I could get this done?" and so on, the coordinator must be able to confidently and sincerely answer those questions.

   Just because a patient tells the doctor that this is the type of treatment she wants and that she doesn't have any questions, doesn't necessarily mean that this is true. She may have all kinds of questions, but is embarrassed or uncomfortable asking the doctor. Patients don't want to look stupid in the eyes of the doctor, and/or they don't want to make the doctor think that he didn't do a good job of presenting the recommendations.

In addition, just because the patient says yes to the clinical dentistry, this doesn't mean that the case is *closed*. The presenter of the clinical aspects of treatment will do the initial close—but the final close comes at the financial presentation. When a patient and the practice come to a financial agreement—an agreement on the total investment and the method of payment, that's the final close. All consultations have two parts: the clinical presentation and the financial presentation.

2.  **In-depth knowledge of money and financing.** The Financial Coordinator must know all about the financial options of the practice, what they are, how they work, and the benefits to the patient. She must be able to discuss money comfortably, handle objections, and not give up until a financial agreement has been established.

    Don't get into a financial discussion only to find that you don't have the materials or the knowledge you need. Your discomfort or lack of preparation will come across loud and clear to the patient. And then, no matter how great your doctor, you could absolutely *blow* this agreement.

    Doctors, don't ignore this imperative aspect of practice health and of your ultimate success. Making financial arrangements is one of the most important *moments of truth* in your practice. Remember, if one more patient per day goes ahead with treatment, that could make a minimum of a $100,000 difference in your practice.

3.  **Ability to complete any necessary paperwork.** Your Financial Coordinator must be able to complete the written financial agreement, handle any insurance issues, manage your healthcare financial program or programs, and do so with confidence and ability. Remember, you falter, you lose. Be prepared!

## Effective Financial Arrangements

To make a comfortable financial agreement, consider the following:

1.  **Privacy.** Remember, the oral cavity is an intimate zone of a person's body, and so is the pocketbook. Therefore, you need to be in a quiet area that provides the necessary privacy. Do not discuss finances at the front desk in front of everyone for the following reasons:

a. A person may become embarrassed and may schedule the appointment but have no intention to come to the appointment. She may not feel comfortable telling you she has a concern about the fee, and she may not want to ask you for financial options for fear that other people will overhear the conversation.

b. HIPAA. Patient privacy is protected when conversations about treatment and finances are done in private. If you do not have a formal consultation area, a small but neat area can be prepared for consultations, like the dentist's private office.

c. Avoid interruptions like people checking in or telephone calls. If there are interruptions during the financial conversation, mistakes can be made, it's hard to focus, and patients can get very frustrated. Or if there are too many interruptions and the conversation becomes impossible, there may be no financial agreement made.

## Personal Note

We recommend that the treatment coordinator join the doctor when he is planning his cases. The coordinator will know exactly what the dentist wants to do, why he chooses a method of treatment, where he wants to start, how many teeth per appointment, etc. The coordinator knows what photography the dentist is going to use for education of the patient. The coordinator is prepared to give him back-up support, and she can prepare for the financial aspect of the case, as well as the scheduling of the appointments. She is as well-prepared to present as the doctor. There are two aspects of every consultation: the clinical presentation and the financial presentation.

Note in the photographs of our Dallas, Texas client, Dr. Ken Hamlett. He has a large monitor on the desk in his consultation area. He has access to all patient information, including stored and retrievable digital images of the patient to whom he will be presenting, and a *library* of all his cases, so that he can show patients *before* and *after* images of similar situations.

# Plan, Prepare, Present.

(Figure 6.1: Preparing the presentation)

(Figure 6.2: Presenting recommendations with the coordinator present)

We recommend that our clients make their presentation of recommendations with the treatment coordinator present. Once he has completed his presentation and is sure that the patient has no further clinical questions for him, he turns the consultation over to the treatment coordinator and excuses himself.

The Treatment Coordinator has heard everything the doctor has said to the patient—and the questions or concerns expressed by the patient to the doctor. The Treatment Coordinator will be present while the doctor is presenting the clinical aspects of recommended care. (Figure 6.3).

The Treatment Coordinator is fully prepared to give the doctor *quality* third-party reinforcement. The Treatment Coordinator will be able to answer possible clinical questions that the patient may not have been comfortable asking the doctor. (The person presenting the financial consultation needs to have clinical knowledge so that she can give this type of backup and so that she can answer, in layman's language, questions that *will* come up during her time with the patient.)

Once the doctor has excused himself, the coordinator takes over. He/she needs to ask the following question before the discussion of finances begins:

> *Carrie, I know that Dr. Hamlett asked if you had any questions and you said no, but I thought there might be something you would like to ask me.*

---

### KEY POINT: All clinical questions must be answered before a discussion of money takes place.

---

Clear any questions about the procedures/treatment, the course of action to be taken, and give statements related to the benefits of the treatment. Make sure this is the type of treatment the patient wants then discuss the fee.

Don't be in a rush. Have time to answer questions and discuss any concerns. Know that the discussion with the Treatment Coordinator might be longer than the discussion with the dentist. That's okay. Without a financial agreement, there is no scheduling of the appointment, and no dentistry will be done! You want a clear, written financial agreement before the discussion is complete, and you will want to have scheduled at least the first appointment.

(Figure 6.3)

---

KEY POINT: Quoting a fee too early may be worse than
not quoting a fee at all.

---

**Trying to close too fast may be worse than not trying to close at all.
How can a patient make a decision about his financial responsibility
before he even knows what he is buying?**

If you are in an office where there is a small team and only one person
in the business office, you can still do this. Pre-block your appointment
book for the dentist's consultation time and the Treatment Coordinator's
time. Knowing in advance that the Treatment Coordinator will be occupied
with a patient discussing finances makes it possible for other team members
to cover the front desk. The Clinical Assistant can check people in and out
during that time. Put a bell or chime on your front door so that he/she will
hear when a patient arrives and, if need be, place a special message on your
telephone so that you can gather necessary data from incoming calls and
can return the calls immediately.

If you have more than one Clinical Assistant, he/she can answer the
telephone. Make sure all people are cross-trained. It is imperative that the
right hand knows what the left hand is doing. **Crossover is a key element
of every job description.**

What you don't want is for the Treatment Coordinator to be interrupted to handle front desk responsibilities or to answer the telephone while he/she is having a private financial conversation with a patient. That's a great way to lose the patient and to lose the case. Ensure the following:

1. **Professional image.** The person making financial arrangements needs to present a very professional image. Sitting down with a person talking about the financial responsibility for dental care needs to be done in a business-like atmosphere. Business attire is appropriate.

2. **Introductions**. In most instances, the patient will already know the person making the financial arrangement. The patient would have met him or her on the telephone and in the business office. Or if a member of your clinical team is serving the role of Treatment Coordinator, the patient may have met her during the initial comprehensive oral evaluation appointment.

   However, if you are in a large office where one person is handling all of the financial aspects of the practice, including the making of the financial arrangements, make sure that appropriate introductions are made.

   "Ms. Jones, this is Jan Davis, my Treatment Coordinator. I have asked her to join us today for our consultation. Jan will be discussing the financing of your dental care and the options we have available for payment. Plus, she will be scheduling your appointments. I felt that it was important she hear what I'm recommending for you. Is it all right with you if she joins us?" No one in our own practice has ever said "no" to that question.

   Note that the dentist not only introduced Jan, but he also told Ms. Jones what her role was in the consultation. In large DSO or corporate situations, the treatment coordinator or coordinators may be performing presentations throughout the day and only interact with patients during these times or situations. Therefore, either an introduction by another team member or a self-introduction is appropriate.

3. **Body language—watch for buying signs.** Another reason to have the Treatment Coordinator join is that he/she can watch the patient's body language for visual buying signs, or signs of discomfort.

He/she can also hear the exchange between the doctor and the patient, and will know what part of the treatment plan he/she may need to revisit. In addition, the patient will not be able to say, "Oh, no, the doctor said I could do this or that." If he/she is sitting in the room, he/she will know exactly what the doctor did or did not say.

The Treatment Coordinator needs to be in the room, but needs to be noninvasive during the doctor's discussion. She/he should not interfere during the consultation, unless the doctor or patient addresses her with a question. However, she/he does need to make notes for reference during her time with the patient.

4. **Call the patient by name—frequently.** During your financial discussion, refer to the patient by name from time to time. The sweetest sound to a person's ear is the sound of his/her own name. Plus, the patient will feel that your time with them is more personalized. This *Ritz-Carlton* type of quality customer service is appropriate throughout the office by all members of the team, but is critical during the intimate discussion of money.

5. **Have all necessary information.** All the appropriate information needs to be complete and in the consultation room during the financial consultation. The Treatment Coordinator will have the treatment plan in hand prior to the consultation so that he/she can calculate the fees, including the expected insurance coverage, if appropriate. He/she also needs to know what the first monthly payment will be if the patient chooses to participate with the healthcare financing program. (SUPPLEMENTAL MANUAL: 6.1)

If a patient expresses a concern about money on the phone, send her information about your patient financing program. Make effort to get her preapproved before he walks in the door. Or, at the initial appointment if she expresses financial concerns, then have her complete an application for your financing program while in the office. You can send the information over the Internet, by fax, or on the phone. In fact, certain companies have developed relationships with some of the major dental software companies and you can gather the financing information within your software. From there, you can complete all necessary information and send the information through the Internet so that you will receive an immediate response regarding approval and amount of credit.

You want to be so well prepared for this appointment that you do not have to figure out information while the patient waits for you. You want to have all the necessary information to make any kind of financial arrangement. You want to have your *ducks in a row*. Being well prepared says, "We want to take care of you, physically and financially." Being prepared says that you are professionals and handle all aspects of your relationship with a patient in a professional manner.

**(Figure 6.4: Making a financial arrangement)**

Have a team meeting to determine the who, what, how, when, why, and where of your financial arrangements. Make sure that you incorporate all the previous six criteria in your discussion and in your protocol. Get all of your paperwork or digital information in order. Make sure that you have the location arranged and that it is conducive to a professionally presented financial discussion.

The person making the financial arrangements will be making the final close of the presentation. He/she has a critical responsibility. If a patient sees the benefits of treatment as presented by the dentist, then the only thing that may prevent the patient from going ahead may be the financing. Have everything work toward the goal of gaining a high rate of case acceptance, including financial acceptance.

## How to Present a Healthcare Financing Program

Pay close attention to the following presentation script. Count the number of benefits I stress to the patient. A person's behavior will be driven by *what's in this for me*. If you intend for a person to accept your offer to become involved with healthcare financing, you must present the program in terms of how that program will benefit the patient. Memorize this script. Practice it with one another. Individualize this presentation to fit your specific situation. These verbal skills have worked for thousands of people and hundreds of practices. Remember, it's not what you say but *how you say it* that makes the difference.

> **BA:** *Ms. Jones, we have a wonderful method of long-term financing right here in our practice. The program is called ABC Financing Program. ABC offers financing for healthcare, dentistry in our case. You apply right here in our office. You don't have to go anywhere. The application is very easy to complete and will take only a few minutes. I'll be more than happy to assist you. We will send your application to the company through the Internet and will know immediately if they are able to offer you a line of credit. Once you have received a line of credit, we can schedule an appointment to begin your treatment. You can finance your treatment with ABC and can spread the payments out over a designated period of time, thus making your payments very small and payments that will fit nicely into your personal situation.*
>
> *Ms. Jones, based on the treatment that Dr. Jameson is recommending for you, your first monthly payment would be approximately $35. It is a revolving payment program, which means every time you make a payment, your next one is less. You've told me that this is the type of treatment you want to receive, so if you can do that for $35 per month, would that make it possible for us to schedule your first appointment to begin?*

## Overcoming Objections

*"An objection is a request for further information, indicating that the person is interested in your proposal."*

— Tom Hopkins, Author of *How to Master the Art of Selling Anything*

Learn how to present patient financing. And, at the same time, learn how to overcome the "normal" objections you will hear. Defuse the negatives that patients may present. Build their confidence in the value and benefit of the program. Acceptance will be in direct proportion to the quality of your presentation.

Here are some common objections you may encounter and suggested verbal skills for addressing them:

### Example

You have been practicing dentistry for a while and your patients have been paying you small monthly payments for ever and ever and ever.

**Business Administrator:** *Mr. Jones, let me tell you about a new program we have in our office. We have found that many of our patients need long-term comfortable financing to handle the financing of their dental care. So, we have listened to our patients and have responded. We now have available in our practice a method of long-term financing called ABC Financing Company. This company has joined our team to provide convenient financing for dental care.*

*You can apply for the financing program right here in our practice over the Internet. You don't have to go anywhere. Once you are extended a line of credit, you can pay for your dental care for a chosen period of time, and your payments will be very small.*

**Mr. Jones:** *What are you talking about? I have been paying Dr. Jameson forever! Why can't I just keep paying him out the way I always have? Doesn't he think I'm good for the money anymore?*

**BA:** *Of course he does. We are still offering long-term payment, just as we have in the past. We are just doing it in a better way. We have been advised by our accountant that it is neither time nor cost-efficient to run a banking business within our practice. We decided it was better for our patients if we concentrated on what we do best, and that is providing excellent dental care.*

*We have become associated with a reputable company that offers long-term extended payments to our patients. This company works with us to offer this convenient financing. In addition, Mr. Jones, we are committed to maintaining comfortable fees for our dental services, and so we have searched for a better, more cost-efficient way to offer long-term payments so that we can keep our fees at a comfortable level.*

**Mr. Jones:** *Well, what is this program? How does this work?*

**BA:** *It's a company that features convenient financing for healthcare. By having a line of credit established for your healthcare, you can comfortably budget this vital service into your monthly income.*

**Mr. Jones:** *I don't know about this. Is it hard to apply or to get accepted?*

**BA:** *You asked a good question, Mr. Jones, and I am glad to tell you that the application is quite easy, and the acceptance rate is quite high. In fact, you apply right here in our office. The application will be similar to any application you have filled out previously. However, if you do have any questions, I'll be more than happy to help you. You can complete the application and send it to the company over the Internet and receive a response immediately.*

**Note***:* Alter these particular verbal skills to fit the requirements of your company.

**Mr. Jones:** *Well, are they going to charge me interest?*

(Response #1 for the revolving payment plan.)

**BA:** *There is a service fee, Mr. Jones, just as you pay with any other financing program. The service fee is 1.75% a month or about $1.75 per month for every $100 that you finance, and Mr. Jones, I'm sure that you will agree, that is not much considering the fact that you can receive the treatment that the doctor has recommended to you, and you won't have to make a major investment all at once.*

(Response #2 for the deferred interest plan.)

**BA:** *Dr. Jameson has paid all necessary fees for you to participate in this program so that you can spread the payments over a designated period of time, and you will not be charged any interest. We need to select a period of time within which you can complete the total payment because, if for any reason, you cannot pay the total fee in the designated time frame, any interest that would have accrued will be added into your remaining balance. That won't change your monthly payments by much, and this is a safety net for you in that if you have an unexpected event that makes it difficult for you to complete the payments, you just keep paying the monthly fee. And, as long as you can keep up with those monthly payments, you are just fine.*

*So, there is no interest charged—except in the situation I just described.*

*That's great, isn't it! Now, let's look at the total investment you will be making for your dental care and determine how much per month is good for you so we can select the option that's best for you. The amount you choose to pay each month will determine the length of time we select. You are only required to pay a minimum payment per month of 3% of the outstanding balance—but, remember, you must have the total fee completely paid by the time frame we select. And, you will be glad to know—there are many options. Tell me, Mr. Jones, how much per month is comfortable for you to pay?*

**Mr. Jones:** *Well, I don't know about this. I just wish I could pay Dr. Jameson the way I used to.*

**BA:** *I know how you feel. We have other good, long-term patients that felt confused about the changes we are making until they found out that they could still spread out the payments for their dental care. However, their monthly payments are usually smaller, and they can take longer to pay their balance. Mr. Jones, we have many families using this program, and they just love the convenience. These families* *seem to be happier because with their available line of credit, they can take better care of themselves and their family on a more regular basis.*

**Mr. Jones:** *OK. So, how much will my monthly payments be?*

(Response #1 for the revolving payment plan.)

**BA:** *You are only required to pay 3% of the outstanding balance. The fee for the treatment that Dr. Jameson has recommended for you is $1,000. Your first monthly payment will be approximately $30. It is a revolving program, which means that every time you make a payment, the next payment will be less. Would that be comfortable for you?*

(Response #2 for the deferred interest program.)

**BA:** *You will be required to make a small monthly payment of 3% of the total balance which would be $30 for your case. Then, you can take care of the balance in any manner you wish as long as the total balance is paid by the end of your agreement. You can choose any length of time between three and twenty-four months to pay. The length of time you select is up to you.*

**Note:** Most companies determine the length of time they will give a patient to pay in full by the size of the charge. For example: for charges of $300 or less, 3 months is maximum; $700, six months; and $1,000 or more, twelve months. There are companies that will go longer—up to twenty-four months with the deferred interest. For a longer payment period, an extended payment program would be appropriate. I'll explain next. Check carefully into the specifics of the various companies and find the one that fits your needs.

In the previous example, I have used a particular set of percentages for illustration purposes. You would have to integrate the specifics according to your own program. But study these verbal skills and scripts. Put these skills into your own words and become comfortable with them. The presentation makes all the difference.

Once your financial system is in place in the practice, everyone on the team must provide support for the program. It is very difficult for a business manager to make financial arrangements with the patients based on the financial protocol, only to have exceptions in the clinical area!

I am not suggesting that the dentist does not have the option to make an exception to a policy. She should certainly have that option. However, the business manager must know that he will be supported and backed up by the dentist and the entire team if your financial protocol and system are going to work well.

If a patient asks a question about financing, money, or cost in the clinical area, here's how to handle those questions.

### Example

**Patient:** *The doctor says I need a crown. How much is that? And how can I pay for that?*

**Team Member:** *Ms. Jones, are you concerned about the financing of your crown?*

**Patient:** *Well, yes.*

**Team Member:** *I can appreciate your concern. We have several excellent financial options available for our patients. Joe, our Business Administrator, handles all financial aspects of care. He's terrific. I'll let him know of your concern. He will discuss the total investment you'll be making, and the options we have available for payment. We have some very convenient methods of financing. I'm sure that you and he will be able to find an option that will work for you. Once you work the financing out with Joe, would that make it possible for you to receive the care that Dr. Jameson is recommending? I know you don't want to lose that tooth!*

**Patient:** *Maybe. I'll have to see what he says. But, yes, I do want to save that tooth. I just need a way to pay for it.*

In the previous dialogue, the clinical team did not close the door on the financial question, but rather, left the door open for the patient and for the Business Administrator. They gave a very positive introduction to the financial option and gave a professional compliment to the Business Administrator. A compliment of this kind from the clinical team can make the financial discussion go much smoother.

Clinical team, you must be careful not to close the door to a positive financial discussion. Don't give the patient the idea that a discussion of money is a taboo thing or that the fees are so high that you wouldn't want to touch such a discussion with a ten-foot pole.

Another option for payment is the Extended Payment Option which lets patients who need extensive care pay for their treatment over a long period of time (24-60 months) at a fixed monthly payment. This option is for implant, comprehensive restorative, aesthetic and surgery cases, etc.

### Example

**Treatment Coordinator (TC):** *Ms. Jones, you've wanted to restore your mouth to health again and be able to smile confidently for a long time haven't you?*

**Ms. Jones:** *Yes, I have! I can't believe I've waited this long to do something about the mess I've put myself into!*

**TC:** *Well, the good news is that you are here, and Dr. Hamlett is just the person to restore both your health and beauty.*

**Ms. Jones:** *I know. He's the best. So, now tell me the news about how much this is going to cost!*

**TC:** *The investment you will be making in your new health and smile is $40,000. How would you like to take care of that investment?*

**Ms.. Jones:** *Oh, dear. I knew it would be a great deal of money, but I had no idea it would be that much.*

**TC:** *How much were you prepared to invest?*

**Ms. Jones:** *I had saved $20,000! But $40,000! Wow—that's twice as much as I thought it would be!*

**TC:** *So, you are prepared to invest $20,000—that's great. How would you like to take care of the portion you were not expecting?*

**Ms. Jones:** *I would just have to pay that out, I guess. Can I do that?*

**TC:** *Sure. How much per month would work for you?*

**Ms. Jones**: *Hmmm. Well, I guess I could handle around $400 or $500. Is that possible?*

**TC:** *Yes. I'm happy to tell you that this is possible. Let's complete the necessary paperwork today and begin the process. Once we establish a line of credit for you, we can schedule your first appointment and begin. We can't start that treatment too soon.*

It's important to find out how much the patient came in prepared to pay. They didn't come in not expecting to pay anything! Then, find out how much they can pay per month. Once you have those two pieces of information, you can make a great financial arrangement.

# CHAPTER SEVEN

# COMMUNICATION SKILLS

*"We know that when people learn to communicate effectively with each other, their lives and their relationships can be truly transformed. Effective communication gives people both a way of expressing their needs congruently and non-blamefully and a way of listening so others feel not just heard, but understood."*

— Dr. Thomas Gordon, Founder, Effectiveness Training, Inc.

Y ou can **LISTEN** your way to case acceptance! Of all the communication skills, listening may be the most important and impactful. People want you to help them find a solution to their financial situation, no matter what that may be. You must be a good listener. Identify wants and needs. The only way to do this is to ask questions and listen. Identify objections or problems to treatment acceptance. You must be able to peel the layers of the problem to determine the core or center. Then, and only then, can you come to a cooperative decision as to how to solve that problem. Be aware that **you** may need to offer *alternatives*, different ways to solve the problem, whether that be a problem of time, money, or treatment option.

---

**A problem is only a problem until it becomes defined. Once it becomes defined, it becomes manageable.**

---

There's your challenge. Define the problem. Then, find a way to solve it. Successful practices, teams, and individuals are not those that are without problems. There is no such thing. Successful practices, teams, and individuals are those who learn to face their problems and find solutions. Then, once a solution is determined, they take action.

# Build a Relationship of Trust and Confidence

Dentistry is a relationship business. You are in the business of working with people emotionally, physically, and financially. You interface with individual differences every day. Each patient's needs, wants, and personalities are unique. You have to be the one who flexes; they are not going to flex for you.

A discussion of money is intimate and very personal. Focus on establishing a relationship with the patient before presenting your recommendations, clinical or financial.

---

**Business experts tell us that people will never buy your product or service unless they have a strong relationship of trust and/or confidence with you.**

---

Without question, if people are going to invest in your services, they must have trust in you and your expertise. After all, you are going to be *in their mouth*, an intimate zone of their body. You are going to be impacting their health or you are going to be changing their smile.

Therefore, from the minute the telephone is answered, to the mailing of the welcome packet, to the initial appointment, to the making of the financial arrangements, and through the completion of treatment, each person on the team has what business calls a ***moment of truth***. *Each person on the team has a chance to make or break a relationship with a patient.* Each step of the patient's path must be based on the establishment and the continuation of trust.

## Engagement

If it is true that each person on the team can make or break a relationship with a patient, then please do not underestimate your importance on the team—no matter what role you have! You are so important, and every interaction you have with a patient can make THE difference as to whether or not the patient moves ahead with treatment, stays with the practice, and refers others to you. You DO MAKE A DIFFERENCE—EVERY DAY!

So, what is this thing called "engagement" that is considered the key element of a successful business?

Here is a definition of ENGAGEMENT from Allegiance, Inc.:

**"The emotional bond or attachment that a client/patient develops during repeated and ongoing interactions accumulated as a satisfied, loyal and influencing customer. Any discussion of engagement must include the relationship between the customer and the employees who are responsible for taking care of the brand."**

(Figure 7.1 Dr. Cappy Sinclair and Team of Virginia Beach, VA, along with his Jameson Management consultants.)

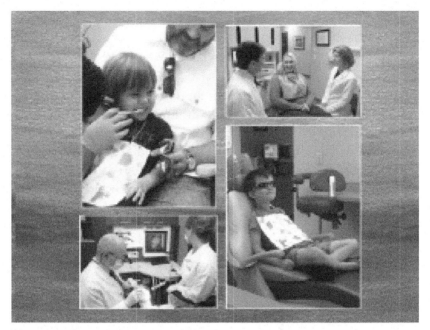

(Figure 7.2)

(Figure 7.3: Jameson Management Clients, Dr. Mark Hyman and Dr. Ken Hamlett and their teams engaged in serving patients.)

Each time a patient is with a member of the team, in that moment, the person they are with IS THE PRACTICE. And that interaction IS THE PRACTICE. The ADA says the main reason a person leaves a dental practice is unfriendly staff! How is that possible? Who would be unfriendly to the people who are paying their salary?

If you are nice to people, they will usually be nice back to you. If someone is being difficult, they probably have something going on in their life and they need help. BE KIND.

## Listen Your Way to Financial Acceptance

Listening may be the single most important communication skill when you are trying to establish a solid relationship and gain insight into personal concerns. Listening can make all the difference.

Here are a few of the things that might get in the way of being able to listen well in a regular dental day:

- Time pressure

- Stress—not being able to relax

- Mindset—being rigid in thought processes

- Talking too much—dominating the conversation as the *authority*

- Thinking what to say in response instead of listening

- Lack of interest

## What Attitudes Are Required for Successful Listening to Take Place?

1. **You must want to hear what the other person is saying.** This takes time. Scheduled time for discussion of financial issues lets you and the patient focus on this intimate discussion without interruption. The patient won't feel rushed and neither will you. You need time if you're going to listen well enough to determine a person's questions, concerns, and particular needs. The point here is vital: you must be able to hear the other person's point of view, determine what she wants, then be able to communicate well enough to address those wants.

2. **You must sincerely want to help the other person with the problem.** The position of Financial Coordinator or Treatment

Coordinator must be assigned to someone who *wants* to work with this area. The best Treatment Coordinators are "challenged" by getting a "yes" to treatment and by finding the right financial solution for a patient.

3.  **You must be able to accept the other person's true feelings.** Other people will have feelings different from yours. Sometimes these feelings may be different from what you think they *should be.* Learning to accept these differences and not letting them affect your relationship may take both time and effort. Don't give up just because you get a "no" right off the bat. Keep trying!

    In the area of financing, you may hear statements from patients that could be offensive. For example, "This fee is ridiculous. What does that dentist want to do, go to Hawaii on my mouth?" and so on.

    I've heard everything and you probably have, too. It may be difficult to accept another person's opinion at first. But as difficult as it may be to listen to the person, letting the patient get things out on the table is step one. Make sure you are clear about their concerns. Only then can you address them—and, hopefully, solve them!

4.  **You must trust that the other person has the ability to handle his/her feelings.** You cannot make another person feel differently. However, you can influence a person's opinion. You want to get the patient to a place where he/she will listen to the options that are available. You can "lead" a person into making a decision—a decision to go ahead with treatment. That's what a good leader does—influences people to make good decisions for themselves.

    The goal of determining open lines of communication is to develop a win-win solution. *The best way to get a patient to listen to you is to listen to the patient first. The better you listen to the patient, the better they will listen to you when it comes time for you to present your financial options.* A good solution is one that works for both parties.

5.  **You must know that feelings can be transitory.** Be accepting of the *human nature* of changing feelings. Don't make judgments about a person based on your automatic reaction. Take the time

to truly define the problem, design a plan for the resolution of the problem, and the implementation of the solution.

Don't prejudge anyone. You may be surprised at which patients accept the full treatment plan. Go into every financial presentation with a positive mindset. Believe every person will accept the treatment. You will have a much greater acceptance rate.

6. **You must be able to actually listen without becoming self-stimulated or defensive**. Allow for a *separateness*. The other person is unique from you and responds in his/her own way. Respect this separateness (i.e., often, when you *hear* what another person says, you *do* become defensive and, thus, close the door to *good communication*). A more effective way to truly *listen* to another is to reflect back to the person what you think you are hearing. By *actively listening* to a person, you are able to get to the center of the message—what the sender really means.

7. **Silence.** Saying nothing at all is just fine, if you are truly *listening attentively*. Silence is a nonverbal message that, when used effectively, can make a person feel genuinely accepted. Ask a question. Then, give the patient your full attention.

8. **Body language**. Body language accounts for approximately 60% of the perception of a message, whether you are sending it or receiving it. Examples of good body language are eye contact, being on the same level, slightly leaning forward, arms and legs uncrossed. If 60% of the perception of a message is body language, then pay close attention to it. Videotape yourself in your various roles and see how you can improve.

9. **Tone of voice.** Tone of voice accounts for 30% of the perception of a message. Be willing and able to reflect the personality of the patient. If they are high energy, step it up a notch. If they are quiet and serene, you may need to soften your conversations. In addition, record yourself. Critique yourself and work on improvement.

10. **Words**. The words you speak account for 10% of the perception of the message. I certainly am interested in the verbal skills, as is evidenced throughout this book. But no matter how excellent your verbal skills, 90% of the message you are sending or receiving is everything but verbal skills.

## Passive Listening

When a person begins to share information with you, encourage continuation by sincerely saying such things as, "Oh," "I see," "really," "uh huh," and so on. These simple, nonjudgmental responses are called "passive listening" by Dr. Thomas Gordon. This passive listening, along with attentive body language will (1) make the patient comfortable, (2) motivate the patient to share information, and (3) develop a trusting relationship that leads to mutual respect.

## Active Listening

The term and concept of active listening was also developed by Dr. Thomas Gordon. Active listening is restating in your own words what you understand the other person to be saying. Active listening gives you a chance to "clarify" or to make sure you heard the person accurately. When actively listening to someone, give careful attention to both the content of the message and the feeling that is being transmitted.

### Example

**FC**: *Ms. Jones, the fee for the recommended treatment is $1,800. Let's discuss our available methods of payment so that we can find the one that best suits your needs.*

**Patient**: *$1,800! You have got to be kidding! For one tooth?*

**FC**: *You seem surprised with the fee.*

**Patient**: *I am. I can't believe that it costs that much to fix this tooth. I just think I'll have him pull it out.*

**FC**: *You came in to see Dr. Jameson because you wanted to save your tooth, but you are surprised by the investment to do so.*

**Patient**: *I'd like to save this tooth, but I had no idea it would be this much.*

**FC**: *Are you concerned about the total fee or about finding a way to pay for this?*

**Patient**: *Finding a way to pay, I guess.*

**FC**: *So, you do want to save the tooth and do see how important this is to your overall health. Correct?*

**Patient**: *Well, of course.*

**FC:** *Great. Then, what we need to do is find a way for you to save the tooth and, at the same time, find a comfortable way for you to finance this so it will not be stressful to you.*

**Patient**: *Yes. If I'm going to be able to get this done, I need a way to pay it out.*

Feedback to the person your own understanding of their message. This type of listening helps to establish clarity. You must know the concern of the patient.

You will shoot yourself in the foot if you begin answering questions before you determine the real problem. Often, the opening remarks are only the peripheral issue. Listening lets you peel the layers of a problem to get to the core, the real issue.

## Don't Become Defensive

Although there may be roadblocks that get in the way of good listening, becoming defensive toward the other person is, perhaps, the greatest barrier.

In order to *NOT* become defensive, the single best skill you can use is listening. According to Dr. Gordon in his book *Making the Patient Your Partner* the following three characteristics describe a good listener:

1. Empathy

2. Genuineness

3. Acceptance

Native American lore says, "You can't walk a mile in another person's moccasins unless you first take off your own." That's a good way to describe *empathy*. The only way to let a person know you are really interested in him, without judgment, is to listen. A person feels important, respected, and validated when you listen.

*Genuineness* means you are congruent or sincere in your willingness to hear what another person is thinking and feeling. It also means you are willing to be honest with your own feelings.

*Acceptance.* You may not agree with what another person says, but you must be able to accept his opinion or, at least, accept his right to express his opinion. This is also a way to express respect for another.

> *"I am best heard and understood when I first hear and understand you."*
> — Author unknown

## Presentation of the Fee

How do you move from the clinical presentation to the financial presentation? How does the dentist keep the doors open for a good financial discussion, but not get involved with that discussion?

Once the dentist has presented the clinical recommendations, he/she needs to ask the following questions:

**Doctor**: *Carrie, do you have any questions about the treatment that I have just presented to you?*

The patient may say no. However, she may say something about money, like the following:

**Patient**: *Well, yes, I do have a couple of questions. How much is this, and how can I pay for it?*

Then, the dentist should answer in the following way:

**Doctor:** *Carrie, are you concerned about the financing of the dentistry?*

**Patient**: *Yes. It sounds like a lot of treatment, and I'm not sure I can afford it.*

**Doctor:** *I certainly understand how you feel. Many patients have felt the same concern until they found out that we do have several excellent payment options right here in our practice. Jan, our Treatment Coordinator, will discuss the total investment and the options we have available. She is excellent, and I feel confident that she will be able to work things out with you. Once the two of you find a financial option that* *works for you, is this the type of dental treatment you would like to receive?*

**Patient**: *Yes. I know I need this. And I want to do it. I just need to see what it's going to cost.*

**Doctor**: *OK. Then, I will excuse myself and let you and Jan work together. I am certain you'll find the right option, and I'll look forward to working with you to get you healthy again.*

The previous discussion is a closing sequence by the dentist that clarifies whether or not there are clinical questions that need to be addressed. It also leads nicely into the financial discussion. It paves the way for the Treatment Coordinator to take over and to do so with the professional compliment from the dentist, thus building the patient's confidence in her ability. The dentist acknowledges the patient's financial concern but does not get involved in the financial discussion.

I do not have a problem with the dentist quoting the fee, as long as the quotation is accurate. However, the Treatment Coordinator needs to be the one who works toward the financial agreement!

Notice the dentist *did* open the door for the discussion by telling the patient there were several financial options available, but the dentist *did not* discuss those options. The dentist needs to get back to the chair. Also, the business person will do a better job, and she will be less vulnerable to requests by the patient to let them pay out their dentistry at $2 per month for the rest of their lives.

Now the Treatment Coordinator changes her location. She can sit where the dentist was sitting before her departure. She needs to be sitting on the same level with the patient and there should not be anything between them like a big desk.

(Figure 7.4)

(Figure 7.5)

**TC**: *Carrie, I know the doctor asked if you had any questions about the treatment that he recommended and you said no, but I thought that there might be something you would like to ask me about the treatment before we discuss the financial responsibility.*

**Patient**: *No. He explained everything just fine. And I could see the problems on that camera. So, hit me with the tough stuff.*

**TC**: *The fee for the treatment the doctor has recommended is $3,000. How would you like to take care of that?*

This is exactly how to present the fee: the statement of the total investment followed by the qualifying question: "How would you like to take care of that?" Then, be quiet and listen to the patient's response. They will give you the direction you need to find the right solution.

**Patient**: *$3,000! You have got to be kidding?*

**TC**: *It seems that you are surprised with that amount.*

Actively listen to the patient to see if you are hearing them accurately. This gives you a chance to clarify. Do not overreact. Do not start "back pedaling" or justifying or becoming defensive. Just listen.

**Patient**: *Surprised isn't the word for it. I'm shocked! I had no idea it would be that much. That's way too much money for teeth!*

**TC**: *How much more is it than you expected?*

The answer to the statement, "That costs too much," needs a responsive question. The Treatment Coordinator wants to know if the whole thing is too much, or if the treatment is just more than had been expected. And she will begin here to determine if the patient wants the treatment but needs a way to pay. Again, with a qualifying question, she gains necessary information to move ahead.

**Patient**: *Oh, about twice as much! I knew it would be quite a bit. I thought it might be around $1,500 or so—but $3,000! WOW!*

Here the question asked by the Treatment Coordinator led to the patient's response that the total investment was the shock—about twice what she was prepared to pay, $1,500. But she will need help with the other $1,500 if she is to go ahead with the treatment.

**TC**: *Carrie, you do want to receive the treatment that Dr. Hamlett is recommending, right?*

**Patient:** *Well, yes. That's what I need. I know that! But I just can't afford that much!*

**TC:** *If I am hearing you correctly, you are saying that you were prepared to pay approximately $1,500 for your treatment, but the additional $1,500 is the real stumbling block. Right?*

Clarification through active listening.

**Patient**: *Yeah. I guess so. I had some money saved for this, but not that much.*

**TC**: *Since you are prepared to pay $1,500 from your savings account, if we are able to finance the other $1,500 so that the investment is not a financial burden for you, would that make it possible for us to go ahead?*

Here the TC is trying to get back to an open line of communication with the patient. She is trying to get past the issue of the total investment and have the patient start thinking of a method of payment that would let her proceed with treatment. If the patient's mind is closed, she cannot hear any further discussion. The mind must be reopened so that a logical discussion can take place. If a person is overwhelmed with emotion, she cannot think logically.

**Patient**: *Well, maybe. What can we do?*

**TC**: *I do want to make you aware of one option that would help you save some money. If there were any way that you could pay for the treatment in advance, we would reduce your fee by 5%. We would not be involved with any bookkeeping, that would save us time and money, and we would be able to pass those savings on to you. In your situation, that would save you $300. That's quite a bit of savings. Does that sound like a possibility?*

You will notice that she closes her statements with a question to get the patient's response and to keep the patient involved.

**Patient**: *No. I have the $1,500 cash, but no more than that.*

**TC**: *You could pay the $1,500 that you have saved, and then we could spread the $1,500 balance equally throughout your treatment. The doctor will be seeing you for three separate visits. We could accept three $500 payments with one payment being due at each of your three appointments.*

**Patient**: *No. That is still too much for me. I have a limited income and can't do $500 at a time. Can I just make payments to you for a while?*

**TC**: *You would like to take care of the $1,500 right now and then spread out the remainder of the fee over a period of time and keep the payments small.*

Active listening!

**Patient**: *Yeah. That's the only way I could do it.*

**TC**: *How much per month would you be willing and able to invest?*

This is a critical question. The TC is, again, qualifying. She needs to ask this question to see which type of payment option she will offer in order to satisfy the patient's need.

**Patient**: *Oh, I was thinking about maybe $40 or $50 per month.*

**TC**: *I am happy to tell you that we do have a couple of options that will let you do just that. We accept all major bankcards. We could place the $1,500 balance on one of those bankcards—whichever one you choose—and then you could pay however much you want every month. Does that work for you?*

**Patient**: *No. I don't want to use my credit cards.*

**TC**: *Then, let me tell you about another option many of our patients have chosen to use. We have an arrangement with a financing company called ABC Financing Company. They offer a financing program for healthcare, including dentistry. You apply right here in our office, right on the Internet. You don't have to go anywhere. The application is easy to complete, and I will be more than happy to assist you. Tell me. How much per month would be comfortable for you?*

**Patient**: *Well, maybe $75-$100 per month. That's it.*

**TC:** *I'm happy to tell you that works just fine. Once they've extended a line of credit to you, you can finance the $1,500, and your monthly payments will be around that amount. So, what I am saying is that you can receive the care that Dr. Hamlett has recommended, and you'll be able to comfortably afford the monthly payments. How does that sound?*

**Patient**: *OK. That sounds pretty good.*

**TC**: *Great. I have an application right here. Let's get going on this.*

Study the verbal skills I have outlined here and throughout the book. Learn how to present a healthcare financing program, and how to overcome the normal objections that will come up. Practice. Practice. Practice. You should be able to answer any objection. The verbal skills should roll off your tongue because you have learned them so well.

Practice so that you will never become flustered because you don't know how to respond to a patient's objection. If you believe in your services and in the payment options you have available, and if you have mastered great verbal skills, you can present with confidence. Increased case acceptance will be the positive result!

Once the financial agreement has been made, write it down. The patient may keep a copy for her own reference and records. File one in the patient's record. Know that just because someone tells you she understands, or that she will remember, doesn't mean that she does or will. Your records will become vital.

Every time a person comes to the office, you will be collecting the agreed upon amount of money. You will also know the method of payment selected and be prepared for the collection process. Once the fee for the day has been collected, remind or reconfirm the patient's financial responsibility for the next visit.

Anyone in the office should be able to access the record of the financial agreement so that if the Treatment Coordinator/Business Administrator, or whoever made the agreement, is out of the office, anyone can note, quickly and accurately, how much is to be collected on each patient, and the method of payment that has been agreed upon. Your digital records are critical.

No one should ever walk out of your door without an appointment either with the hygienist for continuous care or with the dentist for the next phase of restorative care, or in some cases, both. In addition no one should ever walk out your door without paying for the day's service and being very clear about their financial responsibility for the next visit.

## Sample Scripts for Handling Financial Questions

Be ready for patients' questions regarding your financial program. Here are some suggested scripts:

**Example**

**1:** You are no longer handling long-term accounts on your own books.

**Team Member:** *Ms. Jones, we are no longer able to carry accounts here within our office. Our accountant will no longer allow us to manage a banking business within our practice. We have found that in order to maintain comfortable fees for our patients, we must be able to concentrate our time and money on providing great dental care.*

**2:** Patient wants to wait until after insurance has paid to make any private payments.

**Team Member:** *Ms. Jones, I can understand that you want to see what your insurance will pay before you make any investment yourself. However, because we have accurate* *information on your insurance benefits, we are able to estimate very closely what your insurance will cover and the portion for which you will be responsible. Therefore, in order to cover our laboratory and operating expenses, we ask that you take care of your part at the time of the service.*

*We will file your insurance as a service to you. However, if for any reason your insurance company does not pay what we expect, then you will be responsible for the balance.*

**3:** Patient says she doesn't get paid until next week and asks if she can send you a check.

**Team Member:** *Ms. Jones, for your convenience, we do accept all major bankcards. You can place your payment on a bankcard today and pay it off next week when you get your check.*

Or, if you so choose:

**Team Member:** *I can accept a postdated check. I will keep it here and will not deposit the check until next Friday.*

(Collection experts, bankers, accountants, and attorneys that we have contacted all agree on the legality of doing this. Collection experts say that 95–98% of all postdated checks clear the bank.)

**4:** Patient doesn't have her checkbook.

**Team Member:** *Oh, I see. Well, that happens sometimes, doesn't it? We do accept all the major bankcards. Which would you prefer?*

*You don't use bankcards? Well, then I will give you a statement and a self-addressed, stamped envelope. You can send us a check as soon as you get home. We will look forward to receiving that check in a couple of days. I will make a note to myself that we can expect your check. I will inform the doctor of our agreement.*

Make a note in your tickler file. If you don't get the check in a few days, call.

**5:** You have made financial arrangements with a person. He comes in the day of the preparation appointment. When he is being excused from the clinical area, he informs you that he does not have the agreed-upon payment.

**Team Member:** *Mr. Jones, I am confused. We discussed your financial responsibility for this appointment and came to a comfortable agreement. However, since we do not carry accounts on our own books, I would be able to accept a credit card payment today. Then, we will be able to send the models of your case to the laboratory.*

If he doesn't have a bankcard, tell him you will hold the case and as soon as he brings in payment, you will send it to the lab. You will need to complete the treatment obviously, but consider holding the models for a brief period of time as a motivator for payment.

Also, it is a good idea to collect money before a patient is seated. "Mr. Jones, we have a few minutes before we seat you in the clinical area. Let's take care of your paperwork so you can go back to work as soon as the doctor has completed your care."

But, best of all is to go back to the chapter on financial options and try your best to initiate option 1 and 2—full payment in advance with a 5% accounting reduction or cash courtesy before you begin, or half to reserve the appointment and half at the initial appointment.

**Example**

A financial arrangement is made for treatment. The patient is in the middle of the treatment but is not abiding by the financial agreement.

**Team Member:** *Ms. Jones, I became concerned when we didn't receive your payments as scheduled. This may force us to delay your treatment. I know you want to proceed with your treatment. And so, it is critical that we come to an agreement so that you can go ahead with your dentistry. How may I help you?*

**Example:** You have made a financial agreement that is comfortable for your patient and for you. However, the patient has not fulfilled his obligations. You have made consistent efforts to negotiate an agreement but have not received cooperation from the patient. Now you are making your last telephone call before you turn the patient over for legal action. You wish to make one last effort to prevent such action.

**Team Member:** *Mr. Jones, I will be forced to turn your account over for legal action unless I receive your payment in full immediately. I am calling today to discuss this with you in the hopes that we might be able to do something about your balance. I know you want to avoid legal action. So do we. I'm sure you will agree with me that avoiding such legal action would be better for both of us.*

## Verbal Skills to Use When Discussing Financing

As I have said throughout this book, the way you say something makes all the difference in the world, and your success will be in direct proportion to your ability to communicate. There are some words that bring about a positive response, and some that seem to stimulate a negative response. Several of these are listed. Use the positive words and phrases and eliminate the others. This will take practice, but it will be worth the effort.

## Words and Phrases

| Negative | Positive |
| --- | --- |
| money, dollars | fee for the service |
| charge, cost | financial responsibility, total investment, monthly investment |
| bill | statement |
| discount | cash courtesy, fee reduction, or accounting reduction |
| sign here | please initial or may I ask for your signature? |
| policy | financial options or financial protocol |
| deposit | initial investment |
| do you want | Ms. Jones, your fee today is $55. Will that be cash or check today, or do you prefer to use a bankcard? |

# CHAPTER EIGHT

# OVERCOMING THE FEAR OF COST: HANDLING OBJECTIONS

*"It costs 5–6 times more to win a new customer than it does to keep one."*

—Michael Le Boeuf, Ph.D.

You diagnose thoroughly and completely. You prepare for an excellent consultation. You present your recommendations to the best of your ability. The patient tells you this is exactly what they want to do to get healthy again, save their teeth, or have a more attractive smile or all of these. Then, they tell you they can't afford it.

Has this happened to you? Like, every day? Frustration, right? That's why there is so much dentistry sitting in your charts waiting to be done. That's why doctors are so "anxious" about getting more and more new patients, because not enough patients are saying yes to comprehensive care.

If you pay your bills with the "bread and butter dentistry" in your practice and you do one major case per month: (implants, restorative, aesthetic, etc.) that will put you over the top into a nice profitable mode. But that's easier said than done. And as I've said throughout this book, if people come to you, they need or want something. Your major task is to find out what they want. Listen (previous chapter) and then discover the barriers (previous chapter) and FIND A SOLUTION TO THEIR FINANCIAL BARRIERS!

Now let's take an even deeper dive into the realm of handling objections. This is the key to increasing your productivity by 10-40%.

If you wonder what you can do to deal with the objection, the barrier, the fear of cost, the answers are here. The first step is to look within your own mind and heart and find out if you are getting in your own way! Do you have a "fear of your own cost?"

## Are You Worthy?

From dentists and dental team members, we often hear the following comments/statements:

"Our fees are too high."

"Our fees are already above usual and customary. We can't take the fees any higher."

"We live in a low-income area. We can't charge much for our services. No one would come to us."

"The dentist already makes enough money. His wife/her husband just wants more and more and that means we have to work harder and harder to keep her/him happy." And so on. Every day we hear these kinds of comments from participants in lectures, private conversations with doctors or team members, and in our in-office consultations. Each and every one of these comments reflects a lack of self-esteem in terms of being worthy of being paid for services rendered.

As a dental team, have a conversation about the value of the services you provide. Discuss the following questions:

1. What services do we provide for our patients both clinically and otherwise?

2. How do our services benefit the patient—physically, mentally, emotionally, and socially?

3. What would be the down side of a person not having a healthy oral cavity? What if a person had decayed and/or lost teeth, periodontal disease, or an unsightly smile?

4. What would be the up side if these factors were taken care of by our team? Healthy teeth and gums, disease free, and an attractive smile?

5. What do we do in terms of customer service that makes the patient's time with us comfortable, stress controlled, and pleasant?

6. How do we "go the extra mile" to make sure our patients receive all that they expect and a little more each and every time they interact with us?

7. What kinds of business and educational services do we offer that enhance our patient's experiences with us?

8. What makes our practice a good choice when a person is selecting a dental home?

9. Do we understand the financial stresses of our patients and their families? What services do we provide to help them with these concerns so they can receive necessary and desired care? Is this valuable?

10. How do we communicate with our patients so they feel important, valued, and appreciated? Is this worth anything?

11. Who on the team would like to make more money? Why? What would you do with it? How much more money do you need to do that? Is that important to you or your family? Are you worthy of that?

12. What would it take to make that happen? Is it okay for the doctor to take home less money so that everyone else can take home more? Or would it be better if everyone pitched in together so everyone benefited? How can you make that happen? What would be the benefit of that?

Once you have answered these questions, you may discover that you are indeed worthy of being paid well for the services that you provide, and that when patients perceive the value of your services, they will pay willingly. Or you may discover that there are places that need work in your practice, and that in order to feel worthy of your fees, an enhancement of your practice protocols and systems would be beneficial. Invest time and money to elevate your practice to the next level. This will come back to you multifold.

I, for one, do not know anyone who provides a better, more meaningful service to people than dental professionals. I have never worked with people who care more, try harder, provide better care, and enhance people's lives any more than dental professionals. You do not need to apologize for your fees. You do not need to compromise your fees or feel badly for charging people for the treatment they receive from you.

You are a healthcare provider and provide for mankind in a humanitarian way. I hope humanitarianism will always be a part of your life. However, determine how, when, and where you will provide your missionary work. Please, always be willing to do some "just because" dentistry. This "love gift" will come back to you in ways that far exceed any monetary reward. However, you cannot run your practice on a missionary basis unless you are truly, just that. You are running a business, and unless you run that business well, you won't stay in business and you won't be able to provide care to anyone.

Now, let's look at a step-by-step way to handle objections, specifically the objection of *cost.*

## 1. Validate your services and quality to yourselves.

Do you feel that the value of your services exceeds the fee you are charging for it? As I just discussed, before *anything* else happens, you must convince yourself of your own worth.

### KEY POINTS

- Your entire team must believe in the services you are providing.

- You must have a strong commitment to your work and the patients you serve.

- Know that you, as care providers, add value to the lives of those people.

- Make sure the treatment your patients are receiving is an equitable exchange for the fee.

**Exercise:**

**List the services you provide for your patients—from the initial contact through the entire treatment. Now as a team, answer the following questions:**

a. What makes your services *special?*

b. What *added value* touches do you provide that make your practice unique?

c. What do you do that goes beyond the expected?

## 2. Validate yourself to your patients.

You must establish a relationship of trust and confidence with a patient before treatment acceptance will result. Your *ongoing* internal marketing program should have this as its foundation. In planning your marketing/educational program, ask this question, "Does this marketing tool make a statement, consciously or subconsciously, about who we are, what we do, what our purpose is?" If the answer is *yes,* then the marketing tool is probably going to serve your purpose well. If the answer is *no,* then you may need to rethink the project.

## 3. Validate your services.

In your efforts to validate your services to existing and potential clients, do the following:

1. Use testimonial letters from enthusiastic patients. Be sure to include these in your social media.

2. Use before and after photographs of *your* patients to illustrate a particular service you provide. Be sure to obtain written permission from your patients.

3. Provide civic presentations throughout your community using before and after photographs of treatment you have provided.

   a. Concentrate on one subject at a time (i.e., cosmetic dentistry, non-surgical periodontal therapy, preventive dentistry, etc.)

   b. The program must not be self serving, but educational.

   c. Leave a written piece with each participant.

   d. Keep the program short, 20–30 minutes.

   e. Use layman's language.

   f. Using visual aids like Powerpoint is excellent

   g. Be enthusiastic and energetic.

4. Access reviews from your Social Media.

## 4. Make sure every aspect of your practice epitomizes the professional image you wish to project.

All of these foundational efforts work to establish a value for the service that far outweighs the *fee.*

# Handling Objections

I learned from Tom Hopkins that an objection, including the objection of cost, is actually a step forward in completing an agreement. If your patients do *not* pose any objections or raise any questions, they're probably not interested. Now I know that an objection is a gift.

**Four Insights About Objections:**

1. You identify an objection by asking questions and listening.

2. An objection is a request for further information.

3. If a person presents an objection, he/she is interested.

4. Objections are the steps necessary to the close.

An objection is actually an opportunity for you. It defines a specific area of concern or interest. Ask questions to isolate or identify what objections, if any, might get in the way of a person going ahead with treatment.

When an objection is posed by a patient, take the following steps:

- **Hear out the objection.** Don't interrupt. Encourage the person to express himself. Objections often diminish when a person is allowed to talk about it.

- **Actively listen.** Rephrase and repeat back to the person what you think you heard them say. This gives you a chance to 1) clarify, 2) reinforce the patient, and 3) move forward.

- **Reinforce the importance of the objection.** *There's no point in disagreeing or arguing with a patient.* When you listen to the concerns, reinforce those concerns, and share in the development of possible solutions, you will be less likely to see that patient leave without scheduling an appointment.

**Example**

**Patient:** *I don't want to lose my teeth, but I sure don't want to spend this much money if this isn't going to last.*

**Dentist:** *Keeping your teeth for a lifetime is important to you, and you want to make sure the investment you make is going to be one that lasts for as long as possible.*

**Patient:** *Yes.*

**Dentist:** *I totally agree with you.*

**Answer the objection.** Provide further education. Stress the end results and benefits of the treatment you are recommending. Turn the objection into a benefit. Establish value. Use the "feel, felt, found" response:

**Dentist:** *Mr. Jones, I understand how you feel. Many patients have felt the same concern about making an investment in comprehensive dental care, until they found out that an investment in quality, comprehensive care now will 1) provide better health, 2) last longer, 3) look better, and 4) save money in the long run.*

**Confirm the answer.** Get the patient involved with you by asking questions. Then stop and wait for the response. This involvement helps a patient to become an active part of the decision making process.

**Dentist:** *This type of comprehensive care provided now would answer your concern about making a stable, long-term investment, wouldn't it?*

**Change the direction of the conversation and move forward.** Using a phrase, such as by the way, changes the focus of the conversation. Move to another area of interest that will move the conversation in a positive direction. Such as:

**Dentist:** *By the way, Mr. Jones, do you have any particular scheduling concerns we need to be aware of?*

**Close.** Once you have dealt with the objections, ask for a commitment, close. Closing an agreement means asking!

If you don't ask for a commitment, you are giving your patient permission to procrastinate!

**Dentist:** *Mr. Jones, do you have any further questions about the treatment I am recommending for you—any questions about the clinical aspects of the treatment?*

**Patient:** *No. I can see what is wrong and what you need to do.*

**Dentist:** *Then, once you and Jan are able to develop a financial agreement that works for you, shall we go ahead and schedule an appointment to begin?*

**Patient:** *I guess so. Might as well go for it.*

There is the dentist's close. Now the financial coordinator will need to do the same thing. She will reconfirm the dentistry, present the total fee, the options for payment, get a commitment for one of those options or a combination of options, and will close. Then she will schedule that first appointment.

Remember that you control a conversation with questions. When a person poses an objection, don't freeze up and feel that you've hit a dead end. Not so! As you skillfully learn to handle objections you will find that these objections are progressive steps taken to move ahead.

---

**KEY POINT: If you *know* something is going to be brought up as an objection, *you* bring it up. This gives you an opportunity to turn a potential negative into a positive.**

---

### Example

**Dentist:** *Mr. Jones, before I give you the results of my analysis, and before I explain the treatment I recommend for you to reach optimum oral health, first let me tell you that if you have any concerns about the financing of your treatment, we do have convenient, long-term financing right here in our office. I tell you this so that, for now, we can* *both concentrate on your treatment. But please know, we will discuss financial options in full. We want to make sure you are clear and comfortable with this important part of your treatment. Okay?*

## Examples of Closing Sequences

**Dentist:** *And so, Mr. Jones, the financing of the dentistry is a concern for you, is that right?*

**Patient:** *Yes.*

**Dentist:** *When we find a financial solution you would like to proceed. Am I right?*

**Or**

**Dentist:** *Mr. Jones, if I understand you correctly, this is the type of dentistry you would like to receive.*

**Patient:** *Yes, it is.*

**Dentist:** *Then, once we make the financing of the dentistry comfortable for you, is there any reason why we shouldn't go ahead and schedule an appointment to begin your treatment?*

**Or**

**Dentist:** *Now that we have agreed on the treatment and once Jan has worked out the details of your financial agreement, we will schedule your first appointment and go ahead. How does that sound?*

## Learning To Handle Objections

Objections diminish when a person is allowed and encouraged to talk about them. Make sure to:

1. Restate the patient's wants and needs.

2. Actively listen to their concerns. Rephrase and feed back their objections.

3. Validate the person by using "Feel, Felt, Found."

4. Turn the patient's objections around by asking a question to establish value.

5. Encourage the patient to share in the development of a solution.

---

**KEY POINT: If a person is allowed to be a part of a decision-making process, he/she will be more likely to buy into the decision.**

---

You can't push anyone into making a decision, but you can lead them carefully and caringly by asking questions and listening. You can't *talk* people into going ahead but you can *listen* them into going ahead.

## One More Time: Examples of Verbal Skills That Identify and Overcome Objections

A person says, "That's just too much." When a person tells you the fee is too much, actively listen to make sure you're hearing them correctly.

> **Dentist/Business Manager:** *You feel the fee is too high for the services I'm recommending for you? Or is the investment difficult for you at this time?*

> **Patient:** *I'm sure the treatment is worth the fee, but I can't afford this right now.*

> **Dentist/Business Manager:** *Tell me, Mr. Jones, if we can make the financing comfortable for you with convenient monthly payments, would that make it possible for you to proceed?*

> **Patient:** *Probably.*

> **Dentist/Business Manager:** *How much per month could you invest?*

> His answer to this question would let you know if you could go ahead by offering him a bankcard or a HealthCare Financing Program.

**Example**

**1: Patient:** *Well, I want those veneers. I hate my smile. But $10,000 is just too much!*

**Dentist/Business Manager:** *How much more is it than you expected, Mr. Jones?*

**Patient:** *About $5,000 too much—abut twice as much as I thought it would be! I saved $5,000 for this—but, wow, I had no idea it would be this much!*

**Dentist/Business Manager:** *So, the solution we're looking for is a way to finance the $5,000 beyond your current savings, is that right?*

**Patient:** *Yes.*

Now you know that the $10,000 isn't the problem, it's the $5,000 that needs attention and assistance.

**2: Patient:** *I'll have to think this over.*

**Dentist/Financial Coordinator:** *Well, I appreciate that, Ms. Jones. I know you wouldn't take the time to think this over if you weren't interested. So I can make sure I am clear, won't you please tell me, what is it you need to think about? Is it whether or not this is the type of treatment that would be best for you?*

**Patient:** *Oh, no. I know I need this.*

**Dentist/Financial Coordinator:** *Then do you need to think about whether or not I/Dr. Jameson would be the one to provide that treatment?*

**Patient:** *No, if I do this, I want Dr. Jameson to do it. I don't want anyone else to stick their hands in my mouth!*

**Dentist/Financial Coordinator:** *Then, tell me Ms. Jones, is it the money? Do you need to think about whether or not you are able to make this investment now?*

**Patient:** *Yeah. Money is a bit tight right now.*

What happened in this example is that because of careful and caring questioning, the true problem has been identified and can now be addressed. The communication skills here make it comfortable and possible for the patient to say that they need to find a way to pay for the treatment. Many times a patient will say that they need to "think it over," and the dental person with whom they are conversing will just say, "Oh, okay. Well, give us a call when you are ready."

At that moment, the whole issue drops in a bucket. You must identify the patient's problem. You must make it comfortable for him/her to tell you if there is a financial issue. Some people are embarrassed or too proud to come out and tell you that they need some financial help. Let the patient know that you understand the situation, and that you have alternatives. Open doors that historically have been closed.

### Example

**Patient:** *I can't believe I need this much work! How is this possible?*

**Dentist/Financial Coordinator:** *I can't tell you that, Mr. Jones. There are many things that affect your oral health: age, nutrition, what and how you eat, home care, stress. Have you been under stress over the last year or so?*

**Patient:** *Man, have I!*

**Dentist/Financial Coordinator:** *Our responsibility is to evaluate your situation and make a thorough diagnosis based on a comprehensive gathering of data and a complete analysis of that data. Then, after careful study, we make recommendations we believe would help you to get and maintain oral health for a lifetime.*

*You have total control in the decision making. Whether or not you proceed with the treatment that I/we are recommending is completely up to you and the choice is yours alone. However, my/our responsibility as your dentist/dental team is to do the very best job we can to diagnose, create a treatment plan, and*

*present to you a course of action that we believe would be in*
*your best interest. Is that OK with you?*

Tom Hopkins has taught me the difference between an objection and
a condition. My understanding of this difference has been very helpful as I
work with people, whether in the dental office or elsewhere.

An **objection** is a request for further information and shows that the
person is interested in a continued discussion of the proposal.

A **condition** is a situation that is going on in a person's life that prevents
them from going ahead, at least for the moment. Say that a person has just
been released from the hospital and has high bills there, or a person has lost
a job. These are conditions that might prevent the patient from accepting
treatment, but it doesn't mean they don't want it!

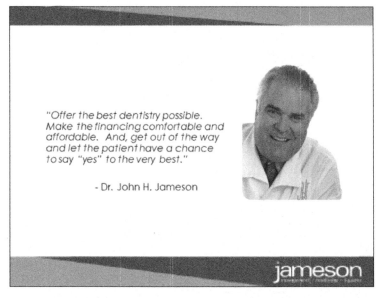

"Offer the best dentistry possible.
Make the financing comfortable and
affordable. And, get out of the way
and let the patient have a chance
to say "yes" to the very best."

- Dr. John H. Jameson

As you are present, ask closing questions that will identify objections or
conditions. If you identify a condition, let the patient know you will be there
when he/she is ready and you will stay in touch. Knowing the difference
between a condition and an objection lets you know where to go and how
to get there. The communication skills for this type of identification are
critical. The very best way to identify a condition or an objection is by asking
questions and listening, actively!

Here is an exercise for you. Practice will give you the necessary
confidence to communicate financially.

1. List the main financial barriers or objections your patients give you.

2. Using skills from this chapter, formulate scripts that will help you deal with and overcome those objections.

3. Role play using these scripts.

4. After role playing, answer these questions:

   a. Did I listen carefully?

   b. Did I repeat what I thought were the patient's main concerns?

   c. Did I validate the patient?

   d. Did I answer each objection with a *values* question?

   e. Did I go through the steps of dealing with an objection?

   f. When I overcame the objections, did I close?

Do not fear an objection, even the objection of money. Rather, look at this as an opportunity. Know that, if you do your best and the person does not go ahead, they are rejecting the treatment proposal. They are not rejecting you. Combine a strong belief in your team and the services you provide with the skills to get that message across. Then you can deal effectively with, "Gee, Doc, it costs too much!"

# CHAPTER NINE

# INSURANCE
# MANAGEMENT

*"Be insurance aware but not insurance driven."*

— Cathy Jameson, PhD

nsurance has been a tremendous benefit to both patients and practices, but is, without a doubt, a double-edged sword. There are frustrations on the part of both patient and practice. Patients would like to have better coverage for needed and desired care, and doctors would like to be paid more equitably for the care they are providing, more in line with their costs, overhead, and Usual and Customary Fees.

A few challenges that practitioners face are as follows: (1) inappropriate increases in yearly maximums by insurance companies or no increases at all. Thus, a patient's insurance plan covers less and less care. (2) Insurance companies that dictate fees, treatment modalities, and/or types of treatment to be covered. (3) Difficult, if not detrimental, communication with the patient about the dentist's fees. (4) Major impact of managed care on the profession.

According to data at the time of publication of this book, approximately 85% of all dental insurance is PPO (Preferred Provider Organization) which is a major change in insurance coverage. Private indemnity insurance is rare. HMO (Health Maintenance Organizations) are also a small division of insurance carriers, and capitation is rarely seen. Four out of every five dentists are accepting at least one PPO. There are fewer and fewer Fee For Service, totally private pay, providers. Most doctors who are totally private pay, meaning that they do not take any insurance on assignment, nor are they providers for any plan, have been that way for a long period of time and have a patient base that are loyal and are used to this manner of pay. These doctors are usually providing very high-end types of care, and people come to them from far and wide because of a very established reputation.

However, for this chapter, let's look at how to manage insurance to the best of your ability, if indeed you are accepting insurance. Let me stress this point, once again, this is not a book on insurance. I am not going to take a deep dive into insurance. I do not want to mislead you. If you are accepting insurance on assignment, please contact our consulting division at info@jamesonmanagement.com or www.jamesonmanagement.com. Our outstanding management consultants are experts in helping practices establish and manage insurance. Purchase and read Dr. Charles Blair's books on managing insurance and on coding. Go to his courses or the courses of Dr. Roy Shelburne. There are many other people who teach on this subject. Go every year and learn. Remember that 50% (or more) of your income will flow through your practice in the form of an insurance check. It is imperative that you manage this system correctly, and excellently!

## INSURANCE: A VERY PERSONAL PART OF A PATIENT'S LIFE!

The way you handle a patient's insurance is important. No matter how good the plan, or how poor the plan, do not be critical of it in front of the patient. This is very personal to them. This is a benefit they have paid for or received from their employer. If you are filing insurance for them, know this is a service you have chosen to provide. No one forced you to do this. Since this is a choice you have made, do this with a healthy heart. It's not the patient's fault if the insurance company doesn't pay well or is difficult to deal with. But if you are filing insurance as a service to your patients, handle this well.

The handling of insurance is a system. It is a system that needs and deserves special attention because, as I said earlier, if you are accepting assignment of benefits, approximately 50%-60% of your revenue is probably coming in the form of an insurance check. Whether you are computerized or not, there are certain criteria that must be in place in regard to insurance. Hopefully you are filing insurance electronically. If you aren't, start now!

## INSURANCE VERIFICATION

Before a patient receives treatment in your office, verify their insurance program. Gather relevant information about the benefit package from a patient's insurance plan. Necessary information to be gathered is as follows:

1. The employer

2. The carrier

3. The phone number

4. The address

5. The contact person

6. The deductible

7. Maximum per year

8. Policy holder and policy number

9. ID number

10. The coverage types—preventive, basic, major, ortho, and other

11. Frequency limitations

12. When they became eligible for benefits

13. The information on the patient/policy holder

## (SUPPLEMENTAL MANUAL 9.1)

### Verification of Insurance

Patient's Name: _____ Insured Name: _____

Patient's Birth Date: _____ Insured's Birth Date: _____

Social Security Number: _____ Social Security Number: _____

Ins. Co. Name: _____

Group Name: _____

Group #: _____

Employee ID#: _____

Mailing Address: _____

Phone #: _____

Contact Person: _____

Eligibility Date: _____ Verification Date: _____

Coverage _____

Benefits paid on: _____

Calendar Year: _____

Fiscal Year: _____ Anniversary Date: _____

Individual Deductible: _____

Family Deductible Maximum: _____

If Fiscal Year, Dates To and From: _____

Dental deductible met?   ☐ Yes   ☐ No

Medical Deductible: _____ Deductible met?   ☐ Yes   ☐ No

Deductible for preventive?   ☐ Yes   ☐ No

Coverage based on UCR? _____ Or set fee schedule? _____

Are X-Rays covered under preventive?   ☐ Yes   ☐ No

Deductible for radiographs?   ☐ Yes   ☐ No

Behavior Management covered?   ☐ Yes   ☐ No

Are periodontics covered under dental? ☐ Or medical? ☐ % of coverage? _____

Is D4381 a covered procedure?   ☐ Yes   ☐ No   Special limitations: _____

Is D4355 a covered procedure?   ☐ Yes   ☐ No   Special limitations: _____

Is D4346 a covered procedure?   ☐ Yes   ☐ No   Special limitations: _____

Limitations on APT after D4346?   ☐ Yes   ☐ No   Special limitations: _____

Are endodontic procedures considered Basic? _____ Major? _____

Orthodontics covered?   ☐ Yes   ☐ No   Lifetime max: _____

Oral surgery covered under dental? _____ Or medical? _____ % of coverage: _____

IV Sedations covered under dental? _____ Or medical? _____ % of coverage: _____

Are Build Ups allowed?   ☐ Yes   ☐ No Explain: _____

Implants (by report) covered under dental? _____ Or medical? _____ % of coverage: _____

Are there any codes typically downgraded? _____

## Coverage Percentages

Preventive: _____ Basic: _____ Major: _____ I.V. Sed.: _____

## Frequencies & Limitations

Prophylaxis: _____ Evaluations: _____

BWs: _____ PAs: _____ FMX or Pano: _____

Sealants: _____ Age limit: _____

Fluoride: _____ Age limit: _____

Missing tooth clause?   ☐ Yes   ☐ No

Replacement clause?   ☐ Yes   Time Period? _____   ☐ No _____

Waiting period for major services?   ☐ Yes   Time Period? _____   ☐ No _____

Initial placement only?   ☐ Yes   ☐ No

Other exclusions or limitations? _____

---

## General Information

Plan allows signature on file?   ☐ Yes   ☐ No

Plan allows assignment of benefits?   ☐ Yes   ☐ No

Plan requires specific company form?   ☐ Yes   ☐ No

Plan accepts standard ADA claim form?   ☐ Yes   ☐ No

Plan requires or recommends a predetermination of benefits?   ☐ Yes   ☐ No

Accept claims that are faxed?   ☐ Yes   ☐ No

*Coordination of Benefits:*

Does plan honor the following rules?

      Birthday Rule?   ☐ Yes   ☐ No

      Gender Rule?   ☐ Yes   ☐ No

      Benefit vs. Benefit?   ☐ Yes   ☐ No

      Standard Method?   ☐ Yes   ☐ No

      Is 100% possible?   ☐ Yes   ☐ No

Remaining Benefits: _____

Date of Last Service: BWs: _____ Pano: _____ FMX: _____

      COE (D0150): _____ POE (D0120): _____

Additional or Unusual Comments: _____

_____

_____

We would prefer that you collect the entire insurance fee before you begin and file the insurance as a service to your patients, if you choose, and let the insurance company reimburse the patient.

## PRE-DETERMINATION OF BENEFITS

Insurance experts say that unless an insurance company 'REQUIRES' a pre-determination of benefits, don't do one. Most patients who ask for a pre-determination do so because dental practices have taught them to do so. Some people in practices are so apprehensive about asking for money that they put this off by saying, "Oh, let's see what your insurance is going to pay, then we can see what we need to do—or see how much you will owe." **That's a stall tactic on the part of the team.**

Insurance companies LOVE stall tactics. According to insurance experts, there are three times to do a pre-determination of benefits:

1. If an insurance company requires it.

2. If a patient requests it (but try to coach them out of needing this).

3. If the patient refuses to accept accountability for the strengths and weaknesses of their dental plan.

Do not introduce this concept to your patients. Do your best to file their insurance to maximize their benefits, but don't let this deter your resolve to help them get healthy.

Of course, we all know that just because a patient receives a pre-determination of benefits doesn't mean, in the end, the insurance company will pay.

If a patient has an extensive treatment plan, and insists on a pre-determination, consider filing the pre-determination but start the restorative. By the time the response is received, you will be ready for the procedure. Make sure you are tracking the pre-determination of benefits as carefully as filed claims. Approximately 50% of people who file a pre-determination of benefits never proceed with treatment. If you are going to accept assignment of benefits, then consider the following:

1. Quote the entire fee and let the patient know they are ultimately responsible for the entire fee, regardless of insurance payment, or lack of insurance!

2. File their insurance as a service to the patient. Take the assignment of benefits.

3. Collect the estimated patient portion at the time of the service. **DO NOT—UNDER ANY CIRCUMSTANCES—FILE THE INSURANCE AND WAIT TO COLLECT THE ESTIMATED PATIENT PORTION AFTER INSURANCE HAS PAID.** This is financial suicide.

4. Let the patient know up front that they are responsible for this account, that the contract is between them and the insurance company. Verbalize and put into writing that if for any reason insurance hasn't paid in forty-five days, the patient will need to pay for the balance in full. Or, if the insurance company doesn't pay at all, they will be responsible for the total amount.

We recommend a written financial agreement. Don't put yourself into a position for a dispute of money.

---

**KEY POINT: Most people never remember that they ever agreed to anything.**

---

# (SUPPLEMENTAL MANUAL 9.2)

## FINANCIAL AGREEMENT

Patient name: _____ Date:_____

We are concerned about your dental health. We look forward to helping you with your dental care. Please remember that your dental insurance is your responsibility, but we can help. Regardless of what we might calculate as your dental benefit in dollars, we must stress the fact that you, the patient, are responsible for the total treatment fee. As a courtesy to you, we can accept assignment of benefit payments from most insurance companies. This will reduce your immediate, out-of-pocket expenditures. The outlined estimate is based on limited information obtained from your insurance company. We allow 45 days for your insurance company to make a payment. After this time, all inquiries (follow-up) on payments due become your responsibility.

| Area/Appt | Recommended Treatment | Fee | Est. Ins. Pmt. | Est. Pt. Pmt. |
|-----------|----------------------|-----|----------------|---------------|
|           |                      |     |                |               |
|           |                      |     |                |               |
|           |                      |     |                |               |
|           |                      |     |                |               |
|           |                      |     |                |               |

**Total**

Financial agreement for your treatment: _____

_____ Fee reduction of 5 % is available if payment for treatment is made in full prior to treatment.
$_____ – $_____ = $_____

_____ Cash or check at time of service

_____ VISA, MC, AMEX or DISCOVER

_____ Healthcare Financing Program

I understand and accept the TREATMENT PLAN above:_____

Date: _____

I agree to the FINANCIAL RESPONSIBILITY for the total fee. The fees listed on this treatment outline will be honored for 90 days from the above date. After that time, the fees are subject to adjustments.

REMARKS: _____
_____
_____
_____

5. Then, keep track of this. If insurance hasn't paid in the agreed upon time frame, or if insurance pays but they don't pay what is expected and a balance remains, call the patient immediately and collect the balance with a credit card or patient financing program, or send a statement with a self-addressed stamped envelope. You may have prepared a pre-authorization form.

6. Use pre-authorization forms consistently. (SUPPLEMENTAL MANUAL: 9.3) You can do several things with this form:

---

## Authorization for Credit Card Use

PRINT AND COMPLETE THIS AUTHORIZATION AND RETURN.
All information will remain confidential

Name on Card: _____

Billing Address: _____

_____

Credit Card Type: _____ Visa _____ Mastercard _____ Discover _____ AmEx

Credit Card Number: _____

Expiration Date: _____

Card Identification Number: _____ (last 3 digits located on the back of the credit card)

Amount to Charge: $_____ (USD)

I authorize _____ to charge the amount listed above to the credit card provided herein. I agree to pay for this purchase in accordance with the issuing bank cardholder agreement.

Cardholder – Please Sign and Date

Signature: _____

Date: _____

Print Name: _____

Return the completed and signed form to the following:

_____

_____

_____

_____

Ó Jameson Management, Inc. 2019

---

a.  Place any balances after insurance pays onto their healthcare financing program or on a bankcard.

b.  Place the full balance onto their financial program or a bankcard if insurance doesn't pay at all.

c.  Place regular payments on the program if they are on a regular program of therapy or treatment, such as orthodontics. Or, this could be used during your accounts receivable transfer if you negotiate regular monthly payments to service their debt.

# CLEARING UP MISCONCEPTIONS ABOUT DENTAL INSURANCE

You may shake your head every day as patients say things about insurance that are totally "off the wall"! They may have been told things by their employer that are just not accurate, or they misinterpreted how their insurance really works. Clarify incorrect information to disgruntled patients. They think you are the bad guy! The following sheet of information is very enlightening to patients and, I have found, very helpful. This doesn't take the place of verbal discussion, but this back-up clearly outlines a bit of information that seems to be helpful. I don't know who originally wrote this, so I can't give credit where credit is due—but it's great! (SUPPLEMENTAL MANUAL: 9.4)

## FACTS REGARDING DENTAL INSURANCE

Dental insurance plays a large role in helping people obtain dental treatment. Since we strongly feel our patients deserve the best possible dental care we can provide, and in an effort to maintain this high quality care, we would like to share some facts about dental insurance with you.

**Fact #1:** Dental insurance is not meant to be a pay-all. It is only meant to be a supplement.

**Fact #2:** Many plans tell their insured that they'll be covered "up to 80% or up to 100%." In spite of what you're told. We've found most plans cover less than the average fee. Some plans pay more, some less. The amount your plan pays is determined by how much your employer paid for the plan. The less he/she paid for the insurance, the less you'll receive.

**Fact #3:** It has been the experience of many dentists that some insurance companies tell their customers that "fees are above the usual and customary fees" rather than saying to them that "our benefits are low." Remember, you get back only what your employer puts in, less the profits and administrative costs of the insurance company.

**Fact #4:** Many routine dental services are not covered by insurance plans.

Please do not hesitate to ask us any questions. We want you to be comfortable in dealing with these matters and we urge you to consult us if you have any questions regarding our services and/or fees. We will fill out and file insurance forms at no charge. We will do this as a service to you.

If we take assignment on your insurance, we feel that 45 days is a reasonable length of time for us to wait for payment from your insurance company.

Thank You!

## INSURANCE OBJECTIONS

People have to want the dentistry before they are willing to pay for it! How you present is critical to overcoming any fee objections, including objections regarding dental insurance. However, when insurance objections do arise, communication skills are the bottom line to your success.

Here are some normal objections/questions about dental insurance and appropriate responses.

1. **"Does my insurance cover this? If it doesn't, I'm not sure I want to get this done!"**

    **Business Administrator (BA):** *Ms. Jones, we'll do the best we can to maximize your insurance benefits. We want to work with you to find a comfortable way for you to finance* *your dental care. We have several excellent options. I am sure that one of them will work well for you. Let's discuss this.*

**Patient:** *OK.*

**BA:** *First of all, let me ask you this, if we can find a way to handle the financial aspect of your treatment, is this the type of dentistry you would like to receive?*

**Patient:** *Yes, but I don't think I can afford it if my insurance doesn't cover it.*

**BA:** *How much could you afford to invest per month?*

**Patient:** *Oh, I could pay maybe $30 or $40 per month, but no more.*

**BA:** *Okay. With the information we have from your insurance company, we estimate that they will cover approximately $1,000. That's your yearly maximum. The total investment for your necessary care is $2,000. That would leave a difference of $1,000. We work with a patient financing organization who helps our patients with the balance of payment that insurance doesn't cover. Insurance, after all, is a supplement to care, not a pay-all. Both are great. But most of the time, patients will need supplemental help to cover the balance that insurance doesn't pay. That's where this company steps in with their support. We can gather a bit of information from you and send it to the company over the Internet and in a matter of minutes see if they can extend a line of credit for you. Once they do, we'll schedule an appointment to proceed. Your monthly payments would be around $30 per month. Would that work for you?*

**Patient:** *Yes. That would be fine.*

2.  **"If my insurance doesn't cover this, why do you say that I need it?"**

    **BA:** *Dental insurance is a supplement to your healthcare. It is not a pay-all. The benefits that are available to you are based* *on the amount your employer paid for the policy. The less he pays, the less you receive. Predefined benefits have nothing to do with necessary treatment.*

3. **"My insurance covers 100% of my dental care. My employer said it did."**

   **BA:** *Many insurance programs say they will pay 100%. What they don't say is that this is a percentage of their fees, not ours.*

4. **"My insurance company says your fees are above the usual and customary! Why are your fees above average?"**

   **BA:** *Our fees reflect our commitment to quality. Insurance companies provide a great service by supplementing your healthcare, but their benefits are not determined by the quality of the care, only on the amount of premium paid less administrative costs.*
   **Or**
   **BA:** *Thank you for noting that, Ms. Jones. We do our very best to provide quality, above-average dental care. The last thing in the world we would want to put into your mouth or the mouth of any of our dental patients is average dental care. And our fees reflect that.*

5. **"This costs too much."**

   **BA:** *Today, most things do. Tell me, how much more is it than you expected?*

   Most of the time the patient will give you an amount that they feel is too much. The amount that is more than they were prepared to pay. If they do this, you will know what amount has become difficult for them and what amount you need to help them with.

   **For example:**

   **Patient:** *Oh, it's about $1,000 more than I thought. I knew it would be a lot, but $2,000?*

**BA:** *Sounds like you were prepared to invest $1,000, but the fee for your recommended treatment is $2,000, so what we need to work on is a way for you to handle the other $1,000 without being financially stressed. Is that correct?*

6.  **Patient:** *"I have to think this over."*

    **BA:** *Ms. Jones, I know you wouldn't take the time to think this over if you weren't seriously interested. Tell me what you need to think over. Is it the dentistry itself? Are you wondering whether or not this type of treatment will help solve your problem?*

    **Patient:** *No, I know I need this.*

    **BA:** *Then let me ask you, are you unsure if Dr. Jameson is the right doctor to provide your care?*

    **Patient:** *Oh, no. I know he's the right doctor. That's not a problem.*

    **BA:** *Then, let me ask you this. Is it the money? Are you concerned about the financing of your dental care?*

    **Patient:** *Yeah, that's a lot of money. I just don't know if I can handle this right now.*

    **BA:** *I can appreciate that. Let me ask you this, if we were able to finance your dentistry, spread the payments out over a period of time and keep the payments small, would that make it possible for you to go ahead?*

    **Patient:** *Probably. What do you have in mind?*

7.  **Patient:** *"I can't believe I need this much. How in the world did this happen?"*

    **BA:** *I understand your concern. Many factors may have affected your oral health. We can't change what's happened up to now, but we can change the situation that exists and restore your mouth to health again. Then, let's mutually commit to keeping it healthy. You'll make an investment now, and then* *we'll work together to insure that investment with an excellent program of maintenance and home care.*

# MORE ABOUT INSURANCE MANAGEMENT

Management systems in the dental practice need to be both time-efficient and cost-efficient. The insurance management system is no exception. Insurance has been, and will remain, an asset to many dental practices.

You have no choice but to file electronically. If you are not already doing so, make an effort to convert now. Carefully managed electronic filing of claims and follow up will lead to an average of a seven to ten day turnaround on all insurance claims. There should be NO 30-day past due claims. Plus, the valuable time of your team members is not going to be wrapped up in filing claims, sending radiographs and support data, and following up for hours while they wait on hold for the insurance company to respond.

## The Rule of 8: Insurance Musts

1. Decide if you are going to accept assignment of benefits or not and manage accordingly.

2. Practice verbal skills and learn to communicate about insurance, including handling objections.

3. Get insurance verifications as quickly as possible, before the patient arrives, if possible.

4. Move away from unnecessary insurance pre-determinations.

5. Collect the patient's estimated portion at the time of service.

6. Make sure everyone understands that they are ultimately responsible for the treatment fee, in full.

7. Develop a "fool proof" system for filing and collecting insurance claims.

8. Make sure you are receiving insurance payments within seven to ten working days and you have no past due claims.

Make it easy for people to pay. Convenience is important to busy people in today's world. Insurance has been a wonderful supplement to people's dental care and to the growth of dental practices. Now more people can use insurance benefits because they have a way to finance the difference after insurance pays. Take good care of this system within your practice.

# WHEN PATIENTS COMPLAIN ABOUT YOUR FEES

*"I've learned that people will forget what you said, people will forget what you did, but people will never forget how you made them feel."*

— Maja Angelou

"Have your fees gone up again?"

No matter where you set your fees, some people will automatically think your fees are too high. Patients don't really know the fees for your procedures. In fact, most non-dental people can't give you an accurate description of most procedures.

## ANALYSIS OF FEES

Very frequently we hear doctors or team members express apprehension about increasing their fees. There are several reasons why people express concern about increasing fees:

1. Patients will be upset.

2. Patients will complain about fees.

3. People will think you are "gouging them."

4. People will go down the street to another practice because the other practice charges less. In other words, fear of losing patients.

5.   Other practices are providers for a managed care program that you are not associated with, and you are afraid your patients will leave you to go to that practice.

These are legitimate concerns. We recommend you analyze fees every six months. I didn't say go up on your fees every six months, although you may need to do just that. I said analyze them and make logical decisions about where your fees need to be placed. Why the regular analysis? To determine if any of your costs of operation and/or costs of a procedure have gone up. If your costs go up but your fees don't, profits are reduced. The one who usually gets a slash in salary is the dentist. Right?!

It is dangerous and inappropriate for anyone on the team to undermine a reasonable and timely increase in fees. If costs of operation have gone up, so must your fees. Dr. Charles Blair of Charlotte, NC, says his criteria for whether to allow a year to go by without raising fees is very simple: "If no staff member requests a raise for a year, the doctor is free to allow his fee schedule to remain unchanged."

When you analyze your fees, you may find that they are just fine. However, if they need to be adjusted three, five, ten percent or whatever, do so. Make sure your fees are equitable and *in line* for your area, and they reflect the quality of care you are offering.

## THE LAW OF SUPPLY AND DEMAND

In today's dental world, we often see practices *so busy* that they are stressed to the max! These practices are trying to get through each of their frantic, stress-filled days, so they can't even imagine putting in the necessary time to *clean up* their systems. The "busyness" of the practice and the day-to-day demands are holding them hostage. They are seeing huge numbers of patients and have a hard time seeing people expediently. New patients have to be *put off* much too long, hygiene patients cannot be seen in a timely manner, major procedures are put off too far into the distant future because the appointment book is stuffed full of smaller appointments—lots of them!

Being *too busy* can begin to squeeze patient time, increase overhead, and produce stress. The dentists and team members need to orchestrate a plan to increase revenue while decreasing both cost of operation and stress. Focusing on the "fulcrum" of the practice, which is thorough diagnosis, careful and complete treatment planning, and well-organized and presented consultations will lead to more comprehensive care, longer appointments, and less stress for patient and provider. And certainly, if you are too busy and can't see patients expediently, then the law of supply and demand is in your favor. Consider increasing your fees. You may lose a few patients over this fee increase, but you will be able to focus more intently on gaining higher levels of case acceptance and getting your practice in control.

Dentists must get out of the *habit* of thinking that high numbers of patients per day is the only way to be productive. It isn't. Consider what we call the Model of Success:

1. See fewer patients each day.

2. Do more dentistry per patient (when and where appropriate).

3. See those patients for fewer visits.

4. Minimize the number of team members.

5. Maximize their talent.

6. Increase the profit.

7. Share the profit.

8. Decrease stress.

## RAISING FEES: WHEN AND BY HOW MUCH?

Dr. Blair has proven to me that the single *best* way to increase practice profitability is to increase fees. If a practice is *full* of existing and new patients, increasing fees by 10% may cause a small percent of patients to go elsewhere. However, if the overhead of the practice is 65%, the practice would have to lose 22.3% of its patient family before bottom line profits would be negatively impacted. (This is based on Eastman Kodak Studies.) If the practice increases fees by 10% across the board without adding other additional overhead items, the *bottom line* profits of the practice will increase over 28.6%. (For practices whose overhead is 65%.) The higher the overhead, the greater the increase to profit margin.

I must tell you that I have recommended 10% increases in hundreds of practices but have *never* had 20 to 25% of the patient family leave. Not if the practice focuses on quality throughout and has invested in great relationships with patients.

If you want to increase profitability by increasing your fees by 10%, you must be prepared for possible negative response by your patients. You must be strong and ready for a *few* people to leave your practice to go to a lower fee competitor. However, I have rarely seen this happen. Everyone on the team, including the dentist, must agree that seeing fewer patients in a day, doing more dentistry per patient, and seeing the patients for fewer visits is a desirable goal. You must believe in the equability of your fees.

The verbal skills of how to deal with patient objections about fees are very important. You don't want people to leave you. You don't want people to be hostile about your fees. How you handle the *very normal* complaints about fees will make all the difference in the world.

### Example

**Patient:** *Haven't you guys gone up on your fees since my last visit?*

**Team Member:** *Yes, Ms. Jones, there has been a slight increase in our fees. Our costs of operation have gone up and, therefore, our fees reflect that. We refuse to compromise the quality of our care, and so, we carefully position our fees to reflect our commitment to the best.*

**Patient:** *Well, it seems like every time I come in here it costs more.*

**Team Member:** *No, not every time. But I can appreciate what you are saying. When the cost of a procedure goes up, we increase our fee in order to cover those costs. We prefer to do this rather than use cheaper materials. Cheap materials produce average dentistry, and Ms. Jones, the last thing in the world that we want to do is put average dentistry into your mouth.*

Every team member must believe the fees you are charging are equitable for the services being rendered. Dr. L. D. Pankey taught us that a fair fee is one where the patient perceives that the service they received is appropriate for the money they invested, and that the doctor and team feel the fee they received was acceptable.

# INSURANCE AND FEES: USUAL AND CUSTOMARY

There is no question that having a patient receive a letter from an insurance company inferring that the dentist's fees are above usual and customary can cause confusion on the part of the patient and is an inference that the dentist is charging too much. This is a prime indication of a third party coming between the doctor/patient relationship. There is no question that any of us would be upset if the patient developed a misconception about the legitimacy of the presented fee.

One other issue can arise. If letters from the insurance companies are sent to the patients, and if the patients call or make a scene in the office, the team members can become gun shy real fast! They begin to think, "Hey, maybe our fees are too high." Or, "Our poor patients can't pay for that treatment if the insurance company isn't going to pay, so maybe we should drop our fees." That kind of mindset and attitude on the part of the dentist or the team members can lead to financial suicide.

The answer to complaints about fees is *not* to lower fees. Upon reevaluation of your fees, your patient flow, your cost of operation, and your desired mode of operation, more than likely your fees are just fine. For the most part, dental fees are equitable and fair, or, they may be too low.

The following steps need to be taken so you can deal professionally with the complaints you are going to get.

1.  Have the entire team practice the verbal skills of handling the patients' objections.

2.  Create a letter that can be sent to patients when a protest about usual and customary occurs. (SUPPLEMENTAL MANUAL: 10.1)

3.  Place a letter into the practice armamentarium to send to insurance companies and to the state insurance commissioner to *protest* their intrusion into the patient/dentist relationship. (SUPPLEMENTAL MANUAL: 10.2)

If a person has come to trust you and your team, they will not leave you for fees if they perceive that the fee they are paying is equitable for the service they are receiving.

You may have some patients who do give you a hard time. Don't think that because one or a handful of patients protest about your fees that you are going to go belly up. Not raising your fees when *your* own costs of operation goes up *will* make you go belly up. And then, who wins? Not the patients, because you aren't in business anymore.

Put a mirror up to your practice. Are you epitomizing quality throughout? If not, make adjustments where necessary. Make sure each and every visit matches your idea of excellence. Then, set your fees accordingly.

# And, FINALLY

**N**elson Mandela said, "Education is the most powerful weapon which you can use to change the world." I am a teacher. My background is in education and I am proud to have taught school to put my dentist husband, John, through dental school. I believe that my background in education has been one of the greatest strengths of Jameson Management. We don't just tell our clients and team members what to do. We are able to instruct and teach them how to do things, and how to do things well so they can carry on when we are not there. Lao Tsu said, "Give a man a fish and you feed him for a day. Teach him how to fish and you feed him for a lifetime." That's what we do. We teach our teams so that we feed them for a lifetime. We individualize what we teach to fit the needs of the unique practices. And, that is what you do with your patients. Individualize the treatment plans to meet the unique needs of each patient. Continue to learn and grow with each day, each week, each year. There is so much to learn. So much to know. So much room for development. I hope you will take the information in this book and make it your own.

Know that your practice is a conglomeration of systems—25 systems. (SUPPLEMENTAL MANUAL: FINAL CHAPTER) Each of those systems must be carefully and caringly developed. Then, all members of the team must be committed to administering the systems consistently. Even though there are times when you must *flex*. Do not let flexing become the norm. If you let flexing become the norm, you no longer have a system. If one of the

25 systems is not working well, that will have a negative effect on all of the other systems.

For example, if you are not collecting what you are producing, you cannot continue to improve the clinical efficiency in your practice because you will not be able to afford new and better equipment and instrumentation. If you are not collecting what you are producing, you cannot afford to hire and pay qualified employees so your team is strengthened. And so on.

You have been given a path for developing a financial system in your practice. We suggested a good, workable financial protocol. Healthcare financing programs were explained, and you have been encouraged to get involved with these programs. I outlined seven ways to build your practice using a healthcare financing program and carefully wrote out verbal skills, lots of them, for the presentation of these programs. I even wrote out possible objections you might, and probably will, hear from patients and ways to overcome those objections.

The area of financing and collection need not be a dreaded/feared/ignored part of the management of your practice. You are providing a fabulous service to your patients. You are a healthcare business, and you must run your business astutely. Getting and keeping control of your finances is good for you and your patients.

Remember, if you do not run a profitable business, you cannot afford to stay in business. Then everyone loses, you and the patients alike. They need you and the services you are offering. *Collect What You Produce!* That makes it possible for you to continue to serve, and it makes dentistry much more fun.

Finally, stress will be controlled for all parties if the strategies of this book are implemented and followed. Stress can be controlled in the dental environment through excellent management and communication.

I believe in you. Believe in yourself. Be the best you can possibly be—*now and forever.* Contact us at www.jamesonmanagement.com. We are here for you!

— Cathy

# Building a Healthy Patient-Practice Partnership

*featuring Jameson Management's*

Cathy Jameson, PhD, Founder and
Carrie Webber, Owner and Chief Communications Officer

In *Building a Healthy Patient-Practice Partnership*, Cathy Jameson, PhD and Carrie Webber, of Jameson Management discuss how to build your practice by partnering with your patients. You will discover ways to engage your patients in a way they will be more likely to accept recommended treatment, pay willingly, and refer others to you.

You will hear these two leading dental communicators role-play key patient conversations and then discuss the psychology behind their words. Jameson and Webber believe that when you partner with your patients, they feel safe and heard. Communication is the bottom line to your success, including the success of your financial systems. This is the way to *Collect What You Produce*.

For a complimentary copy of *Building a Healthy Patient-Practice Partnership*, please contact www.jamesonmanagement.com.

Made in United States
North Haven, CT
21 February 2022

16357996R00095